MEMOIRS OF A HOPEFUL PESSIMIST

A Life of Activism through Dialogue

DEBBIE WEISSMAN

KTAV PUBLISHING

URIM PUBLICATIONS
Jerusalem • New York

Memoirs of a Hopeful Pessimist:
A Life of Activism through Dialogue
by Debbie Weissman

Copyright © 2017 Debbie Weissman

Typeset by Ariel Walden

Printed in Israel
First Edition   **31088100947207**

ISBN 978-965-524-2652

Published by

KTAV Publishing   Urim Publications
527 Empire Boulevard   P.O. Box 52287
Brooklyn, NY 11225   Jerusalem 9152102, Israel
Tel. 718-972-5449, www.Ktav.com   www.UrimPublications.com

Library of Congress Cataloging-in-Publication Data
Names: Weissman, Deborah, author.
Title: Memoirs of a hopeful pessimist : a life of activism through dialogue / Debbie
    Weissman.
Description: Jerusalem ; New York : Urim Publications, [2017]
Identifiers: LCCN 2016044449 | ISBN 9789655242652 (hardback)
Subjects: LCSH: Weissman, Deborah. | Jews, American—Israel—Biography. | Jewish
    women—Israel—Biography. | Jewish educators—Israel—Biography. | International
    Council of Christians and Jews. | BISAC: RELIGION / Judaism / General. | BIOGRAPHY
    & AUTOBIOGRAPHY / Religious.
Classification: LCC DS113.8.A4 W46 2017 | DDC 296.3/96092 [B] —dc23 LC record
    available at https://lccn.loc.gov/2016044449

Dedicated to Memory

Table of Contents

A Curse and a Blessing

NOT MANY JEWS IN THE WORLD have positive things to say about the World Council of Churches (WCC). Over the years, they have been accused – I would say, sometimes, unfairly – of antisemitism or at least anti-Israelism. But I feel that I owe them a great debt of gratitude. In June of 1988, through the WCC, I underwent a life-transforming experience.[1] They invited approximately sixty women from all over the world, representing nine different religions, to a week-long conference in Toronto, on religion, politics and feminism. Blu Greenberg of New York, a well-known Orthodox Jewish feminist and certainly a respected friend and mentor of mine, suggested that I be invited. When, as a student, I lived in New York before coming to Israel, her husband, Rabbi Irving "Yitz" Greenberg was "my rabbi." He was my role model for integrating particularism and universalism.

Blu had known me primarily from Jewish feminist activities; I hadn't yet done much interfaith work. A year or so earlier, I had begun teaching introductory courses about Judaism to Christians at St. George's College, an Anglican-run ecumenical study center in East Jerusalem.

---

1. A shorter version of this story appeared in my article, "Let each people walk in the name of its god . . .": On Inter-religious Dialogue and Pluralistic Jewish Education, included in Gillis, Muszkat-Barkan and Pomson (eds.), *Speaking in the Plural: The Challenge of Pluralism for Jewish Education* (2014.) It appears here with the kind permission of the Magnes Press, Hebrew University, Jerusalem.

From left, Blu Greenberg and author at interreligious
conference in northern Greece, 1996

Yehezkel Landau, a long-time peace activist, had been their one Jewish
teacher. But he was leaving the country for a semester and asked if I
could take over for him. I told him that I'd never taught Christians
before and I wasn't sure I knew how. He reassured me, and I agreed to
try it. It turned out that I loved it. To my good fortune, when Yehezkel
came back, the College kept us both on.

The nine religions represented at the Toronto conference were Judaism, Christianity, Islam, Buddhism, Hinduism, the Sikh and Baha'i
faiths, Native American Indian spiritual traditions, and the Wiccan
religion. This neo-pagan faith includes witches who practice "white"

The author with a Hindu participant at the
WCC Toronto conference, 1988

magic, nature worship, fertility rites, Druid traditions, and lots of love. I
should note that there were eight women present at the conference, who
were there officially as Jews. There was an additional Jew who came as a
Buddhist and another who identified as a Wiccan. Thus, all together out
of 60 participants, there were ten Jewish women! Considering that the
Jews are less than two-tenths of a percent of the total world population,
that was rather amazing.

The first morning of the conference was devoted to introductions.
We were each given three minutes to introduce ourselves to the whole
group. That year was the beginning of the First Intifada and, being the
only Israeli at the conference, I worried about how I would be received.
I decided to introduce myself as "a religious Zionist who believes that
the best fulfillment of Zionism will come when there is a Palestinian
state alongside the State of Israel." (I still believe that.)

It worked. During the break, many women came up to me in the
women's room or at the coffee table and expressed their pleasant sur-

prise or asked me what I meant by that. I had broken the ice. My major contribution to the conference was being on a panel about the Israeli-Palestinian conflict, with a Palestinian Quaker and a Lebanese Roman Catholic nun. I called for an end to the Occupation, and at the time I said that for me a symbol of peace would be when the Hebrew University and Birzeit University would co-sponsor a seminar on what really happened in Israel in 1948.

But, I added, for the time being, let's not dwell on the past, let's look to the future: we all want a better future for our children and grandchildren. What can we do to bring that about? And certainly one of the most important things is to end the Occupation. I would say the same thing now, except that one of my Jewish colleagues at that conference said to me, "Don't forget history." I don't think I was forgetting history, but now, in retrospect, I think that the achievement of peace *will* involve perhaps not recognition or acceptance, but at least an acknowledgement, of our different narratives.

The entire conference was vegetarian, in an attempt to respect the food-related practices of the various groups. As someone who grew up in a Jewish home in mainstream Christian America, I had always felt that keeping the Jewish dietary laws – keeping kosher – was strange or at least different; Christians don't have rules like these. It is true that during the period of Lent that precedes Easter, some Christians, particularly the Orthodox, refrain from eating meat or some other animal products – as was once customary every Friday – but there is no one food that is defined as "forbidden" to Christians all year long. Because of that, I thought that our dietary laws were a bit strange and were simply *hukim* – laws we follow without any further rationale or explanation.

But then I began to meet Muslims, Hindus, Buddhists, and members of other traditions. In most of those religious cultures, if not all, there are rules that limit the consumption of certain foods. Muslims don't eat pork, Hindus don't eat beef, many Hindus and Buddhists are vegetarians; Jains, adherents of an ancient Indian religion, are total vegans who won't eat even onions or garlic, because eating them involves pulling their roots out of the ground, which the Jains perceive as an act of violence. A friend I met later through WCC-related work is a Hindu physician who lives in South India. She told me that she once coordinated an international, inter-religious youth conference, in which she had to accommodate the dietary needs of many groups. When I asked her if the Jews were the most difficult to accommodate, she replied that it was the Jains. But in the end, she succeeded with all of them.

All of these groups are expressing their religious and spiritual values through their consumption of food, or lack thereof. Thus I saw that in this regard, it is the Christians who are the exceptions among members of the various faith-communities.

Perhaps an even more significant commonality among the women in Toronto was that they all had narratives of suffering. Each community has its own stories of persecution, either in the distant past, the present or, sometimes, both. The Native Americans spoke about their conquest by white settlers; even the Wiccans described their history of witch hunts, trials and burnings at the stake. Of course, a more important question is: what do the groups do with these stories of collective suffering? Do they tell the story over and over again and continue to view themselves as victims, or do the stories become a spring-board for positive action, being sensitive to the suffering of others, healing? Do they promote xenophobia or empathy?

Finally, each religious group was given a time slot – morning or evening – in which to share with the rest of us some prayers or rituals that typify their community. The Jews were given Friday evening. Putting together a *Kabbalat* Shabbat service and then the Shabbat table ritual with eight Jewish women, including Modern Orthodox, Conservative, Reform and Reconstructionist, was in itself no small feat. Despite our own intra-religious differences, we did succeed in organizing a candle-lighting ceremony and abbreviated *Kabbalat* Shabbat service. Friday morning, we went around to the other groups with a question and a request. The question we asked, mainly of the Muslims and Hindus, was: if we also provide grape juice, would it be offensive to you if we had wine on the table? The answer they gave was, "No, but thanks very much for asking." The request was preceded by an explanation that it is our custom to sing at the Shabbat table, so that if the groups had any songs from their traditions that they wanted to share with the rest of us, we would be happy to photocopy the words in advance.

We began the meal, of course, with blessings over the wine/juice and the *hallot*. I was seated next to an Episcopalian nun. I off-handedly remarked to her that she could relate to blessings for wine and bread. Several women had prepared songs and in the middle of the dinner, we all got up to dance. We ended up doing Punjabi folk dances, the Punjab being the origin of many of the women, specifically Hindus, Muslims and Sikhs. When it came time for *Birkhat HaMazon*, the Grace after Meals, we did parts of it in Hebrew and parts in English. One of the lines we said in English was towards the end, "*HaRahaman*, May the Merciful One, make peace between the Children of Isaac and the children of Ishmael." A Muslim woman came up to me with tears in her eyes and said," I never thought I'd hear Jews say that."

During the evaluation session of the conference, a great many participants – mostly non-Jewish women – reported that the highlight of the conference for them had been the Shabbat. The nun I had been sitting next to said the highlight of the week for her was my casual remark (which I had already forgotten) about wine and bread, as it had made her aware of the Jewish roots of her Christianity. For me, the highlight, I suppose, was meeting so many wonderful and impressive women from what to me were exotic places. Compared to the African and South Asian women in their beautiful, colorful garb, I always felt underdressed and bland. While on the subject of clothes, I will relate that in November of 2004, I attended a conference in a town called Soderskoping, south of Stockholm. The K in Swedish is sometimes pronounced Sh, so Kirsten can be Shirsten. Soderskoping I think means "southern market town" and is pronounced "Sodershopping." The conference had about 150 participants from all over the world, men and women of many different faiths and some with none. The theme was "Tools for Peace." During the conference, it snowed. In November in Sweden, that isn't such an unusual occurrence. Many of the delegates ran out to play in the snow, some for the very first time in their lives.

The local newspaper featured on its front page a photo of an African woman and a Southeast Asian man, playing in the snow. What struck me were the vivid colors of their garb together with their dark skins, against the backdrop of the white snow and the grey sky. But they must have been very cold.

Back in Toronto, there were many challenging moments, not the least of which was our experience on a field trip to a Chinese Buddhist Temple (we also visited a mosque and a synagogue – they are all on the same street and share a parking lot). There was a Thai anthropologist at the conference, a lovely, dynamic woman who prostrated herself in front of a huge golden statue of Buddha. I had never seen anyone do something like that before and wasn't sure how to react.

As I noted above, this week was life-changing for me. It set me on a path that led to my further involvement in inter-religious work, including much with the WCC. I have been to many conferences since, but I don't think I've ever attended a conference quite like this one. Usually, the most important part is the informal contact over coffee and meals. In Toronto, every morning I awoke eager to attend the sessions themselves.

In what way did this experience transform me? Growing up in the United States, I had always had Christian friends. But I had made a conscious decision in 1972 to move to Israel and work in the field of Jewish education. For the first sixteen years of living in Jerusalem, I knew relatively few non-Jews locally. Through my work in Diaspora Jewish education, I had met people from throughout the world, but they were all Jews. The women's conference in Toronto put me on a trajectory that led to my devoting years to inter-religious dialogue in general and Jewish-Christian dialogue in particular. Now, when I plan a Shabbat dinner or a Pesach Seder, I almost always invite some Christians.

During the summer of 2014, I realized – and this could be a morbid thought, but in my case, it isn't – that when I die, my stories will die with me. Unless I write them down . . . I have lived through a very interesting time, including the 1960s and 70s. Of course, the Chinese have a curse that says, "May you live in an interesting time." I feel blessed.

In a recent New York Times crossword puzzle, which I do daily, the clue was "unlikely memoirist." The answer was "amnesiac." Perhaps I am also an unlikely memoirist, not having achieved the level of fame or accomplishment that some have. But at least, thank God, I'm not an amnesiac. I wouldn't call this a memoir as much as a collection of short stories. That really happened. To me or to people who were close to me. And here I will share some of my stories . . .

Purim and Palestinians

I LOVE THE JEWISH FESTIVALS. I have taught about them, in English and in Hebrew, to Jews and Christians, young people, teachers, clergy, and Jewish Agency emissaries going abroad.

Every one of the festivals contains two elements that we might call "theory" and "practice." "Theory" would be the story and/or the meanings and ideas of the festival; "practice" would refer to the ways in which we actually celebrate. Some of my good friends dislike the "theory" of Purim, some the "practice" and some, both! (How people who don't enjoy having fun, drinking, acting silly, etc. can be my friends, is a mystery that goes beyond the scope of this short piece.)

With regard to the "theory," I can more easily understand how they feel. After all, the Scroll of Esther, read or, rather, chanted, on the Jewish festival of Purim, appears to be a violent and anti-feminist story filled with revenge against the Gentiles. Chapter Nine lists body counts of the slain. Many people also do not see any connection between a story of the deliverance of a Jewish community in Exile and the carnival-like atmosphere in which the deliverance is celebrated.

To be fair, a number of tragic events happened in the 1990s on or around Purim, which made it increasingly difficult for some Jews, especially in Israel, to continue celebrating as before. The first of these was in 1992, when the Israeli Embassy in Buenos Aires was blown up. Twenty-nine civilians, including four Israelis, were killed in the attack and 242 additional civilians were injured. The second was in 1994, when Baruch Goldstein, a Jewish settler, went into the Cave of the Makhpela in Hebron and took revenge on Palestinians for such atrocities, by himself massacring 29 Muslim worshippers and wounding 125 others. In 1996 and 1997, there were terrible bombing attacks in Tel-Aviv on Purim. In the first case, 13 were killed and 130 wounded; in the second, 3 were killed and 48 wounded. It's no wonder that for many people, the day has very negative connotations.

Nonetheless, Purim happens to be my favorite Jewish holiday. It probably all started when my Bat Mitzvah in 1960 was held on Shabbat *Zakhor*, the Shabbat preceding Purim.

I am also aware of the dangerous potential of this holiday. Even the rabbis in the Talmud were aware of this danger, as we can see in a Talmudic passage (*Megillah* 7a): Said Rabbi Sh'muel the son of Yehudah, "Esther sent a message to the rabbis, saying, 'Make me (my festival) a fixed date in the calendar, for all the generations.' They sent back to her, 'But you and your story arouse ill-will against us among the nations.' She sent back to them, 'But I'm already written in their chronicles!'"

According to this passage, Esther understood the power of her story to arouse ill-will. Her argument was simply that the story was already known. Purim throughout Jewish history was often an opportunity for Jews to vent their understandable anger and frustration at the surrounding nations. One can say that the Book of Esther immortalizes a dream of the Exilic Jew: ". . . and it shall be turned to the contrary, so that the Jews shall rule over their enemies."(9:1) Unfortunately, in February of 1994, a Jewish settler on the West Bank acted to actualize his fantasy:

"Even in hard-line Kiryat Arba, Baruch Goldstein was considered extreme. He was a disciple of the far-right rabbi Meir Kahane, who had been assassinated by an Arab terrorist in New York in 1990. Kahane created a Jewish theology of vengeance and rage. The purpose of the Jewish people, he had preached, was to defeat Amalek – the Biblical tribe that attacked the Israelites in the desert and whose evil essence passes, in every generation, into another nation seeking to destroy the Jews. When Jews erase Amalek, God's name will be glorified and the Messiah will come.

The ultimate Kahanist holiday was Purim . . . The holiday is the story of triumph over Amalek."[1] Haman, the villain of the Purim story, is a descendant of Agag the Amalekite (cf. Esther 3:1 and I Samuel 15:8).

---

1. Yossi Klein HaLevi, *Like Dreamers*, HarperCollins Publishers: New York, 2013, p. 486. I thank Yossi for his permission to use the quotation.

The Amalekites who appear first in Exodus 17: 8–16, are characterized in Deuteronomy 25:17–19 as the ultimate enemy who symbolizes cruelty and evil.

On the surface, Purim commemorates the rather strange sequence of events described in the Book of Esther. In ancient Persia, a megalomaniac leader (Haman) convinced a foolish king (Ahasuerus) to allow a massacre of all the Jews. Through the intervention of the king's adviser, Mordekhai, and his beautiful niece, Esther, who had been chosen queen in a beauty pageant, the evil was averted or, more correctly, the Jewish community was granted permission to defend itself. The story progresses through palace intrigues, as well as a series of banquets and parties. At the end of the book, Mordekhai and Esther declare a festival for the Jewish people to celebrate their salvation from destruction. In the Jewish Masoretic tradition, this is the only book in the Hebrew Bible in which the name of God isn't mentioned, even once.

The story can be analyzed as a paradigm for the Jewish Diasporic experience: assimilation, antisemitism, relations with the authorities, responses of the community to distress, self-defense. Indeed, the Encyclopedia Judaica lists over one hundred special, local Purims. For hundreds of years, whenever a Jewish community felt a sense of release from impending disaster, it declared a local celebration, using Purim as a model. Since one of the important responses in times of trouble is Jewish solidarity ("Go, *gather together* all the Jews . . ." Esther 4: 16), the commandments of Purim, which include giving gifts to the poor and portions of food to our friends (Esther 9:22) are commandments which promote social solidarity.

One of the major customs on Purim is dressing up in costume. The Hebrew word for "to dress up in a costume," is "*l'hithapes.*" Since "*l'hapes*" means "to search for" and the prefix "*hit*" is used for reflexive activities we do to ourselves – to get dressed, to get washed, and so on – we could say that to put on a costume is, literally, to search for oneself. In order to dress up, we have to know who we are, so that we will dress up as who we are not. Or, perhaps, as who we would like to be? Or, even, as who we really are deep down inside – the self that doesn't get much of a chance for expression during the rest of the year?

On a certain level, the festival is really about identity – personal, as well as group – and the relationship with the Other. One of the ways to relate to the Other is, quite literally, by getting into his shoes. Or, perhaps by confronting the Other within ourselves.

Thus, we may even say that Purim is both the most particularly Jewish of all our festivals, and the most universal. It is particularly Jewish because, as mentioned, it reflects the Jewish experience in Diaspora. Mordekhai is the first person in the Bible to be called "*Yehudi*," with the meaning of "Jew," and not just with the meaning of "someone from the tribe of Judah" – after all, he was from the tribe of Benjamin. No longer "Hebrew" or "Israelite," but "Jew."

On the other hand, the "practice" of Purim most clearly reflects non-Jewish and even pagan festivals. Costumes, masks, drunkenness, dancing, laughter, fun – all these remind us of the Carnival or *Mardi Gras*, which occur roughly around the same time of the year. They also remind us of what anthropologists have called "rituals of role reversal" among African or other tribes. Is this purely co-incidental? Is Purim really at its core a seasonal festival to mark that uncertain, even sometimes anxious time that isn't exactly the end of winter or the onset of spring? What is it all about – a deeper spiritual reality, identity and the Other, uniqueness and assimilation, universalism and particularism? I would say, "All of the above."

A well-known rabbinic dictum, not originally mentioned in connection with Purim, maintains that: "A person's character is evident through his anger (*ka'aso*), his cup of drink (*koso*), and his pocket (*kiso*). Some say also his playing/laughing" (Talmud *Eruvin* 65b.) Unfortunately, the alliterative nature of the Hebrew – *ka'aso, koso, kiso* – is lost in translation, but still, we can take this statement and apply it to Purim. We'll go in reverse order: With regard to playing and laughter, Purim is the quintessential occasion for Jewish humor, and the origins of the modern Hebrew and Yiddish theater lie in the satiric *Purimshpiel* (Purim play) frequently staged as part of the holiday celebration. The "pocket" – *kiso* – of the Jew is evident in the outpouring of charity and gifts (see Esther 9:22). Drinking – *koso* – as we said earlier, is mandated, but hasn't generally led to violence or other unacceptable behavior. But we did say that there is a strong element of historic anger – *ka'aso*. How is that to be dealt with?

The tradition of Purim provides us with a wonderful model of how feelings of aggression, even when justified, can be channeled in a non-destructive way. There is a Biblical commandment to "blot out the memory of Amalek" (see Deuteronomy 25:17–19). At first glance, this seems to be, God forbid, a prescribed genocide. But the way Jews fulfill the commandment of wiping out the memory of Amalek is that when the Book of Esther is read in the synagogue on Purim, we make noise at every mention of Haman's name. What a wonderful way to sublimate feelings of anger and aggression. If only all of us could find such creative ways of dealing with frustration . . .

In 1990, I received an invitation from the World Council of Churches to attend their special convocation on JPIC – Justice, Peace and the Integrity of Creation – to be held in Seoul, South Korea. When I opened my calendar, I saw that if I were to participate in this meeting, it would involve being in Seoul over Purim. Now, some Orthodox Jews don't make any important decisions in their lives without consulting a rabbi; I am not one of them. I knew that I wanted to go to this event, but I wondered how "to do" Purim in Korea. There would certainly be *some* rabbis who, when hearing my question, would shudder at the thought and tell me not to spend so much time among the Gentiles.

So I approached a friend, an Orthodox rabbi based in Israel, prominent in inter-religious circles. He began by saying that this is a wonderful opportunity and that he even feels slightly envious. (I assume that by now he *has* visited South Korea.) We sat together and went through the various laws of Purim, such as the gifts to the poor and the portions of food, and explored how to do them in a place with so few Jews. As it turned out, there was at the time an Orthodox rabbi serving as chaplain on the US Army base in Seoul. I made contact with him and part of the problem was solved, although his community was very small and for certain key experiences – such as reading the Scroll of Esther – we didn't have the *Minyan*, the requisite prayer quorum. But it was certainly better than nothing.

At the Convocation itself there were about 750 Christians. There was a small group of about twenty to twenty-five "inter-religious guests": two Jews, and several each of the following: Muslims, Buddhists, Hindus, and Sikhs. We were treated as a special group and were hosted at a vegetarian dinner. I don't eat food that is cooked in non-kosher pots, even if the ingredients themselves are kosher, so vegetarian meals are largely wasted on me. In those days, I used to bring my own food with me to these gatherings. When some of the Muslims heard that I had kosher meat with me, I gladly shared it with them.

I do have a story related to food. Right before Purim we mark the Fast of Esther. It is observed from sunup to sundown (like Ramadan, but we have only four days like that during the course of the year, not a whole month). When it was time to break the fast in Seoul, I went to the dining room, where the dinner buffet was being served. I had brought with me from Israel a can of gefilte fish, and I took a good deal of the fresh salad from the buffet. I sat down to eat and a Christian gentleman from Japan sat down across from me. I thought he was looking at my plate and then he asked, "Where are you from?" I answered, "From Jerusalem, Israel." He then asked, "Are you Orthodox?" I thought to myself, "Wow – he's good!" I thought he realized from what I was eating that I'm keeping strictly kosher and I said, "Yes." "Greek Orthodox?" "No, Jewish Orthodox." "I never heard of that. How many of you are there?" "I replied, "About a quarter of the population of Israel."

Somehow, I think that to this day, he still doesn't understand across from whom he was sitting. But I'm convinced of one thing – it had nothing to do with the food on my plate. There *are* many Greek Orthodox Christians in Israel, and that was a good guess. The obsession with food is a Jewish obsession.

The two Jews who were invited to attend the Convocation, both residents of the southeastern corner of West Jerusalem, didn't exactly represent a wide spectrum of the Jewish people. My colleague, whom I knew from before, is definitely to the left of me both religiously and politically, but on many levels, we're quite similar in our approach. At this meeting, we actually functioned more as Israelis than as Jews. What I mean is that this was during the First Intifada, and it was important for us to make good contacts with the Palestinian Christian and Muslims who were there. Several of them boycotted us; others were open to dialogue.

We met with those who would meet with us and agreed that we would work together on a joint statement, to be read to the entire group on the last night of the meeting. We had several working meetings during the Convocation to put the statement together.

That year, Purim was Saturday night and Sunday. I spent Shabbat in the home of the Army rabbi and stayed for the *Megillat Esther* reading on Saturday night. We made plans to meet with our Palestinian interlocutors later that night in the hotel lobby. Since it was Purim, I ordered a round of drinks for everybody. The meeting went reasonably well. When we finished, it was quite late at night. I went back to my hotel room and turned on the TV. They were showing "The Tonight Show" from New York and one of the guests was an Israeli singer, Ofra Hazah. I took that as a positive sign. Of course, it might have been simply an amusing coincidence.

The Convocation was expected to produce a summary document. In its original version, the draft contained several references to what it called the biblical concept of *Shalom* as representing both peace and wholeness. Bur one of the Palestinian clerics objected to the use of a Hebrew word in the document and so it was deleted. My Jewish colleague and I spent a chunk of our last day at the Convocation painting two flags – an Israeli flag and a Palestinian flag. He asked me to never mention to anyone that he did that, since he isn't much of a flag-waver.

But on the last night of the Convocation, Palestinians and Israelis stood on the stage, next to each other, waving the two flags, and presenting the following statement to wild applause:

> We, as representatives of three religions from our common Holy Land . . . seek to derive from the prophetic and liberating values of our traditions and faiths a way to fulfill the national aspirations of both the Palestinian and Israeli peoples in peace with justice . . . we commit ourselves to work for the following goals:
> – An end to Israeli occupation and an end to the violation of human rights.
> – No further building of Israeli settlements in the occupied territories.
> – Mutual recognition and self-determination for both peoples through negotiations.
> – Sovereignty for both peoples through the recognition of a Palestinian State in the Palestinian homeland alongside the State of Israel.
> We call upon the churches to foster dialogue between Palestinians and Israelis and to combat anti-Arab and anti-Jewish stereotypes. We also call upon the churches to encourage peace initiatives and to join us in common prayers and deeds for peace.
> "For, behold, I create Jerusalem a rejoicing, and her people a joy . . . the voice of weeping shall be no more in her, nor the voice of crying . . .
> And they shall build houses, and inhabit them, and they shall plant vineyards, and eat the fruit of them. They shall not build, and another

inhabit, they shall not plant and another eat . . . They shall not labor in vain nor bring forth for trouble . . . they shall not hurt nor destroy in all my holy mountain," says the Lord (Isaiah 65:18–25).

Two and a half years later, the Oslo process began. We were ahead of our time.

Women's Dialogue for Peace

EVEN EARLIER, I had been involved in a dialogue process of Israeli and Palestinian women, with other women from North America, Europe and the Arab world. In May of 1989, about sixty of us were invited to Brussels for a conference over a weekend. The conference was entitled, "Give Peace a Chance." It was underwritten by the wealthy Belgian-Jewish Susskind family, who generously supported many left-wing projects involving Israel and the Palestinians. There were about fifteen women in the Israeli "delegation;" most were secular Israeli women, including such prominent political figures as MK's Shulamit Aloni and Naava Arad. Three of us were religiously observant – Professor Alice Shalvi, Janine Lazare and me. We made plans to obtain kosher food and spend at least the meals on Shabbat together. The one non-Israeli woman who joined us for Shabbat dinner was legendary Congresswoman Bella Abzug, whose campaign slogan had been, "A woman's place is in the House." It turned out that she had received a better-than-average Jewish education in her youth and fit right in around the Shabbat table, knowing the various table rituals and songs.

At one of those meals, I spoke to the other three women about the Torah portion for that Shabbat. It was *B'hukotai*, Leviticus 26:3–27:34, which contains what is called the blessing and the rebuke. In 26:17, the rebuke includes the phrase, ". . . and you shall flee, but there will be none pursuing you." Based on that verse, I said, one of the greatest curses is paranoia. We have to get over our fears and be open to making peace with our enemies.

Since then, I have had many occasions to quote the one-liner, "Just because you're paranoid doesn't mean they're not out to get you." Even paranoiacs can have real enemies. The Jews today are like paranoiacs who have real enemies. But in those days, things still seemed a bit simpler.

Over the course of the weekend together, we worked on and produced a statement, called the "Brussels Declaration," very similar to the one quoted above. The outlines for peace in this region have been well-known for decades. The question has not been what *should* or *would* it look like, but rather what *could* it look like. Can we achieve it? How do we get from here to there?

All the sixty or so, but one, signed the document. The one hold-out was MK Arad, bound by her Labor Party discipline which – at that point – prevented her from signing in favor of a Palestinian state. Of course, when Yitzchak Rabin became Prime Minister, and as part of the Oslo process, the Labor Party changed its position. But then, perhaps because we were "just women," our statement had very little impact, at least in Israel.

I met some very impressive Palestinian women during that meeting. One of them was Professor Suad Ameiry who, at the time, was a professor of architecture at Bir Zeit University. She said something that I have quoted many times since: "All of Palestine is my homeland. But we must learn to make a distinction between homeland and state; I will be content to have a Palestinian state in part of my homeland." I told her that I could say the same thing about the Land of Israel as my homeland. And I added that if we really had peace, she and I could visit those parts of our homeland that weren't in our state. Now, years later, I wonder if we couldn't also *live* in those parts of our homeland that are not in our state. If the Palestinians and at least some of the settlers would agree to that, it might be a solution to one of the thornier bits of the conflict. As of 2015, I know some settlers who would be willing; I haven't heard yet of any such Palestinians.

A powerful memory for me from the conference was our last meal together, on Sunday evening, in the Susskind's spacious, beautiful home. During the meal, the wine flowed freely, which showed me that the Palestinians who were there were either Christians or secularized Muslims. As we entered, one of the Palestinian women was sitting at the piano. She began playing a melody, very familiar to the Jewish women as the folk song "Rakefet" in Hebrew or "Margaritkelech" in Yiddish. Apparently, it is also a Palestinian folk song. This led to a whole evening of song, dance and good fellowship. Alice Shalvi remembers that at one point, the pianist played "Hevenu Shalom Aleichem." This may sound corny, but we ended the evening, locked arm-in-arm, singing together, "We shall overcome; we shall live in peace." Evenings such as this one have helped to sustain my belief that we *could* achieve some kind of peaceful co-existence. We share so much in common. It's precisely because I love my people and our land that I can appreciate their love for their people and their land.

The next day, the conference was over, but several of us traveled with Alice to the medieval town of Bruges, a fairly short train ride from Brussels. Alice served as our tour guide there and impressed us all with her broad knowledge of medieval history, literature and art.

Four years after that conference, in 1993, from the time it was announced on the radio that Israel was involved in secret talks with the PLO in Oslo, to the famous handshake between Rabin and Arafat on the White House lawn, exactly fifteen days elapsed. At that point, I had a conversation with a colleague who is a professor of political science at the Hebrew University in Jerusalem. I said to him, "You know that I've been hoping, praying and working for this moment for decades. But just fifteen days to go from being each other's worst enemies to a handshake and a signed statement at the White House? Isn't that a little quick? Don't the people on both sides need time to get over their fears and anxieties, break down their stereotypes, and get to know each other as human beings? Wouldn't it have been better to declare that we were talking with each other and then have an actual process – in which Palestinians would be invited to speak in the Israeli media, schools, synagogues, community centers; Israelis would appear in Palestinian media, schools, churches, mosques; there would be grass-roots dialogue, and then, after a few months, the leaders could meet and shake hands?"

To which my friend replied, "I can tell from this that you're an educator and not a politician; politicians seize the window of opportunity."

We were both right. He was right on two counts: Politicians *do* seize the window of opportunity and I *am* an educator and not a politician, which at the time I thought was a put-down; now I take it as a high compliment. But I also think that I was right, that one of the problems with the Oslo process is that there really was no process, on the grass-roots level. One of the greatest flaws of Oslo was that it was almost exclusively secular Israeli men talking with secular Palestinian men. There are two questions here: whether something is lost by not involving women, and whether something is lost by not involving religious people. It has been my experience that women on two sides of a conflict often find it easier to dialogue than do their male counterparts. This is not necessarily due to some innate, essential difference. I believe it is a result of women themselves having been marginalized in society and thus being able to better communicate with each other.

Not long after that, a group of about 150 Israeli peace activists from Jerusalem, including quite a few observant Jews, travelled to the West Bank, to Mt. Gerizim, near Nablus (Sh'chem), for a picnic with Palestinians. It was during the week of Sukkot, when we are supposed to eat our meals in a Sukkah, a temporary hut-like dwelling or booth. Our group brought with us some boards and tools to erect an even-more temporary Sukkah for our lunchtime. The Palestinians were mostly Muslims, and, as distinguished from many dialogue settings in which our interlocutors were academics and professionals, these were "just plain folks," grass-roots supporters of peace. We assured them that we were not on our way to building a new settlement.

But when I tried to explain to three young women among them the religious significance of the Sukkah, and I mentioned that many of our group are religious Jews, they responded, "If you're religious, then it means you're against peace."

The academic year of 1995–1996 was most eventful for Israelis. November saw the assassination of our Prime Minister Yitzhak Rabin; several months later, a spate of bus bombings that led to the first election of Netanyahu. In November, shortly after the murder, and then again in May, the Ecumenical Institute at Tantur, overlooking on the one side Jerusalem, and, on the other, Bethlehem, sponsored a series of interfaith encounters among women. Tantur is a Christian ecumenical center under Roman Catholic auspices – it's affiliated with Notre Dame University in Indiana. I have taught at Tantur since 2000. The women at the conference represented two nationalities: Jewish and Palestinian-Arab, and four religious traditions: Jewish, Christian, Muslim and Druze. The Arab women included both Israeli citizens and Palestinians from the Occupied Territories. I brought my mother to the conference

Author (third from left) with Jewish, Christian and Muslim participants
in WCC Assembly, Bhusan, South Korea, 2013

Author, as director of Kerem Institute for Teacher Training in
Humanistic-Jewish Education, with guest, Cabinet Minister Rabbi
Yehuda Amital, appointed after the Rabin assassination, 1995

in November – I believe it was her first experience in dialogue with Palestinians.

The first day of the deliberations was devoted to "How does my tradition present me with obstacles as a woman?" But the second day was devoted to "How does my tradition empower me as a woman?" I had the privilege and the challenge of appearing on the second panel. Someone called my approach close to that of the Jesuits. I took it as a compliment.

Between the first and second meetings of the group, my mother died.

Zeide and Bobbie

I WAS THE ONLY ONE of the five grandchildren really to have known my maternal grandfather. He died when I was six years old. The next oldest grandchild was my sister Judy, who was only three at the time. I was told later that he kept my picture in his breast pocket and would show it proudly to anyone he met. The affection was mutual, because many years after he died, I spent an entire therapy session crying for his loss.

I know that as a six-year-old, I wrote a book. It was called "Chapters out of My Life." But during our many moves from home to home, the book seems to have been lost. I can't remember now what I could possibly have written about – also, did I write it before or after my grandfather's death? Was that one of the "Chapters"? I'll never know.

I also later found out that as a Jewish boy in early 20th century Poland, my Zeide, as we called him in Yiddish, would spit when passing by a church. I feel that my life, through my work and relationships with many Christians, has been a *Tikkun*, a kind of reparation for him.

Several years ago, I was invited by the then Lutheran bishop-elect of Jerusalem, Dr. Munib Younan, to his investiture, at the Church of the Redeemer in Jerusalem. At the beginning of the service there was a procession of bishops from throughout the world. As they walked past in their official garb, with their lavender shirts, I realized that I knew personally at least four of them. I could hear my late grandfather, nodding his head and saying, "Debbie, it is most essential that you cultivate these friendships. You never know when it might be important for the Jewish community to turn for help to the bishop." Except that now,

Author's maternal grandfather, Jacob Dobzinsky

the shoe is on the other foot. Living in Jerusalem as a member of the sovereign majority, I have had occasion to use my contacts with Israeli government officials to try to help Bishop Munib and his Palestinian congregants.

In January of 2001, the Israeli Foreign Ministry sent me on a lecture tour to Poland. I gave twelve lectures in four different cities in six days. I talked about Judaism and Israel. As many people know, there is a great deal of interest in Jewish culture and a lot of philosemitism among non-Jews in Poland. One of the cities was Lodz, pronounced by the locals as Wuj. My Zeide had come from a town near there.

Author speaking at Poland-Israel
Friendship Society in Warsaw, 2001

The Church, which used to be part of the problem, is now part of the solution. They sponsor a "Judaism Day" in their institutions (this practice began in Italy and has spread as well to Austria and perhaps a few other places). Each year, the central event of Judaism Day takes place in a different major city and is broadcast on Polish television. In 2001, it was in Lodz.

The broadcast featured an inter-religious service held in the Lodz cathedral. They had chosen one of the Psalms, which are not only part of our shared Scripture, but also our shared liturgy. A Jew read the Psalm in Hebrew and gave a Jewish interpretation (in Polish). A priest read it in Polish and did a Christian interpretation of the Psalm, also in that language. There were beautiful musical renditions of Psalms from the two traditions.

We then went across the road to a seminary, where we held a colloquium at which I spoke, and ate dinner. There was a table of kosher food. I was introduced to the Archbishop of Lodz. I thought of my grandfather, who wouldn't have believed that his granddaughter was in Lodz, eating a kosher meal and chatting with the Archbishop.

Both of my grandparents grew up in Poland. They either married and left for Germany in 1919 or married in Germany or perhaps never formally married at all. But sometime during 1920–21 they landed in Canada and crossed the border into the USA, illegally. How can I oppose "illegal immigrants" when, were it not for them, I might never have been born?

A powerful story that my mother told me about her father goes back to the 1930s, when she was a teenage student in the Yiddish afternoon school called *Mittelshule* (middle school). She wanted to quit, but Zeide said to her, "*bei mir qvit men nit.*" It was a bit of a strange combination of Yiddish and English, but he got across the message that "*We* don't quit." A few years later, when my Aunt Rita wanted to quit, he allowed it. I suppose he was stricter with his first-born daughter – this is an example of what a friend of mine calls, in a cute biblical reference, "the Plague of the First-Born."

I'm happy that my mother didn't quit, and I thank my lucky stars that I grew up in a Yiddish-speaking environment. When I was working on my doctorate at the Hebrew University, I took a class called Advanced Yiddish: Reading Texts. There were about a dozen of us in the group, each from a different background: Israeli, American, Canadian, French, Belgian, Mexican, etc. The instructor was Argentinean. Whenever we came to a new word, he would ask us, "And how did your grandmother say this?" This was in recognition of the fact that our grandparents had come from different parts of Poland, Lithuania, Russia, Romania, and so on. To this day, I'm an advanced Yiddish student. My comprehension is excellent, my speaking is OK, but I know no grammar.

In 2014, I enrolled in an intensive Yiddish course offered not far from my home in Jerusalem. We were tested to determine our level, and I was put in the advanced class, although much of the time, I felt I was at the bottom of that class. We were ten students. Four of them were non-Jews (two Germans, a Pole and a Russian.) They tend to be graduate students and/or archivists in the field of European Jewish studies. I'm fairly sure that everyone in the class, except me, had taken basic academic classes in Yiddish and had a grasp of the grammar. My problem was that the terms "accusative" or "dative" weren't meaningful to me even in English. I think Hebrew might not have them. My advantage, as one of the students told me, was that I speak "autentisch." One of the other students was a Sabra Israeli, the daughter of a British immigrant. Knowing English and Hebrew well gave us both an edge in terms of our vocabulary. But I knew the most about Judaism and Jewish texts including Aramaic words and phrases that are used in literary Yiddish.

In fact, one of our teachers shared with us a story about an outstanding Yiddish student whom she had taught, a young woman from Japan. She read a long passage and the teacher asked her if she had understood it. The student replied, "Yes, all except for one word, which is repeated a lot. What is this 'Shabbos'?"

My Bobbie Fela, who was Zeide Yaakov's wife, became widowed in her 50s, when Zeide died of abdominal cancer. I know that some people call their grandmother "Bubbie." But we called both of ours "Bobbie" – Bobbie Fela and Bobbie Ina. I think it might reflect different dialects of Yiddish.

Bobbie Fela was quite a character in her own right. I owe much of my Jewish identity to her influence. She had a deeply pock-marked face and was not physically attractive in any sense of the term, but possessed a certain charisma. Or, at least, charm. Bobbie used to bring all kinds of people home from the park. Once, a gentleman caller she brought home turned out to be an antisemite, who started ranting and raving in her kitchen.

I mentioned earlier that Rabbi Yitz Greenberg had been my role model for finding the right balance between the particular and the universal. I could just as easily have said my grandmother. Both of my grandparents – or, in a certain way, all four of them, plus my parents – were committed to the concept of *K'lal Yisrael* – Jewish solidarity, that the Jewish people is one people and that all Jews are mutually responsible for one another. We are like an extended family throughout the world. Zeide Yaakov was honored by an American association for Polish Jews for having worked during the War years to save Jews and bring them to America.

But Bobbie Fela perhaps most embodied for me the balance I often use in my teaching, taken from Hillel in *Mishnah Avot:* "If I am not for myself, who will be for me? But, if I am for myself alone, what am I? And, if not now, when?" I sometimes paraphrase this to adapt it as a motto for the Jewish people: "If we are not for ourselves, who will be for us? But, if we are for ourselves alone, what are we? And, if not now, when?" Fela was deeply committed to the Jewish people, but also to the rest of humankind. She educated her two daughters, my mother and my Aunt Rita, in that liberal direction. In 1968, a major controversy arose within the Jewish community in Forest Hills, Queens, NY, around a proposal to build a low-income housing project in the neighborhood. Unfortunately, many of the largely white residents of the neighborhood opposed the project for various reasons that included a desire not to open up the area to an influx of African-Americans. I remember that Rita and her husband, my Uncle Harold, were just about the only people in their synagogue who supported the proposal. I was very proud of them.

It was a tiny family. Both Sylvia, my mother, and Rita, my aunt, married only children. I had all together one aunt and one uncle (by marriage). Rita and Harold had three sons who were our only first cousins. Sylvia and Nahum had two daughters, who were their only first cousins. Growing up, I envied people with larger families. My cousin Jay is probably the closest I have ever come to having a brother. His wife, Cindy, is at least as much a part of our family as anyone who was born into it.

The most powerful story I can remember about Bobbie Fela is from 1970. Soviet Communism was a terrible system, but coupled with historical antisemitism, it was an even more dangerous combination. The Jews of the Soviet Union were being denied their basic rights, and movements were springing up all over the West to struggle for their freedom. Singer-actor Theodor Bikel had just issued a phonograph record with songs and stories smuggled out of the Jewish *Samizdat*, the dissident underground in the USSR. The songs, in Hebrew and Yiddish, were full of Jewish pride and Zionism and I was sure that my grandmother would love it. I bought it for her as a Chanukah present and put it on the record player.

The song I was sure she would like best was "*Hai–Hai – zoln zey geyn in d'rerd arein – hai – hai – freilich zoll bei Yidden zein – Am Yisroel Hai!*" The expression, *Am Yisroel Hai*, means, literally, "the people of Israel lives." The rest of the line means, "May our enemies go to hell, and may we, the Jews, rejoice." I played it for her and she said, "I don't like it." "Bobbie, "I said, "what do you mean, you don't like it? I got it especially for you."

"I don't like it, and, what's more, I don't think it's very Jewish. We don't say, 'May our enemies go to hell' – after all, they're people, too."

Author's aunt and uncle, Rita and Harold
Goldberg, at their wedding in 1952

I'm so grateful for this story, because this delightful and amazing woman began to develop Alzheimer's around that time, a disease that would torture her and the family for the next decade, until her death in 1979. After a few years and some frightening incidents familiar to anyone who has had experience with this terrible malady, for example, wandering around in the street without clothes – my aunt and uncle, who were living next door to her in New York, decided, with a heavy heart, that she had to be institutionalized. They put her in a home where she was well-cared for, but her situation deteriorated even more rapidly – again, an experience known to people who take care of aging parents or grandparents. I was one of the last people in the family to see Bobbie Fela alive. During my last visit, she uttered three intelligible words in Yiddish: "*shrecklich*," "*geferlich*" and "*teier*." They mean, literally, "shocking," "terrible," and "dear" (in both senses of the word). I guess we'll never know what she meant.

Young Judaea
and the Year Course

FROM THE AGE OF NINE or so, until I came to live in Jerusalem, I suppose you could say that I was a card-carrying Zionist. Although both my parents had been in *Habonim*, the Socialist Zionist youth movement affiliated with the Israeli Labor Party, or its European equivalent, where we lived in Massachusetts the movement to join was Young Judaea. At that time, it was co-sponsored by two adult Zionist organizations – the ZOA, which was more or less centrist, but has since become very right-wing; and Hadassah, the women's Zionist organization that is ostensibly apolitical, but leans to center-left in Israeli and perhaps also American politics. These two organizations ended their partnership on the American Zionist Youth Commission in 1967, which some of the youth experienced as a kind of parental divorce.

During the years (1962–1977) I was involved with National Young Judaea and its national camp, Tel Yehudah, along the banks of the Delaware River, near Port Jervis, New York, we were the largest Zionist youth movement in the U.S. We claimed a national membership of 16,000. We had been founded in 1909, in America, and were not really affiliated with any Israeli political party. It was a movement that was pluralistic religiously and ideologically and fairly centrist politically. The stated educational goal of Young Judaea was "to develop generations of American Jews, rooted in their heritage and dedicated to attaining 'self-fulfillment' as Zionists." Some of the Israeli emissaries thought this was ludicrous; how could anyone stay in America for generations and still achieve Zionist self-fulfillment? They thought that the only reasonable way to be Zionist was by making *Aliyah*, moving to Israel. It wasn't until 1967, after the Six-Day War, that our movement was prepared to declare *Aliyah* as its chief educational goal. Before 1967, it was considered completely acceptable within the movement to stay in the U.S., be a supporter of Israel, and become a rabbi, Jewish educator, or lay leader.

The other Zionist youth movements, which had their historical and ideological roots in Europe, accused us of being bourgeois and, as they put it, "wishy-washy," and boasted that they were the true Zionist pioneers. I remember that in camp one day in 1963, we had an exchange program with another camp in the area that belonged to the *Hashomer HaTzair* movement. This was a secularist, Socialist youth movement, with European roots, aligned with the most left-wing Zionist Party in Israel. The name, literally, means "the young guard." The members of *Hashomer HaTzair* were educated to make *Aliyah* to kibbutzim affiliated with the movement in Israel. I remember meeting 12-year-olds (I was 16 at the time) who could tell me what kibbutz they would be living on in the future and what work they would be doing. I felt sorry for them, for their doctrinaire ideology. They probably felt sorry for us because we were so open-ended and vague.

That same summer of 1963, during Visitors' Day at the camp, I saw many parents who had Auschwitz numbers on their arms. Only eighteen years after the Holocaust, it was the first time I had seen this. Later that summer, the Young Judaea movement voted to send two representatives to the march on Washington. There they heard Dr. Martin Luther King, Jr., deliver his famous speech, "I have a dream." In retrospect, not only am I sorry that I wasn't one of them; I realize that this event was part of many in my youth that emphasized the lack of a contradiction between Zionism and humanistic values.

The first time I visited Israel was in December of 1964, as a senior in high school. I was serving as National President of Young Judaea and was invited to be a youth delegate to the World Zionist Congress. At 17 and a half, I was the youngest of all the delegates. Of course, in those days, you could have white hair and still be part of a youth movement.

That trip wasn't the greatest I've ever taken. Much of the Congress was boring. I was the youth delegate on the committee for education and culture – a strangely prescient choice – but I don't feel that I had much of an impact. During a free day, a friend of mine who was on

The author, at 17, 1964

the 1964–65 Young Judaea Year Course took me up to Mt. Zion in the heart of Jerusalem. From there, we could catch a glimpse of the Old City, behind the walls. Going up, we had seen a sign warning us not to take pictures. As an American teenager who had never experienced a conflict zone (unless you count the dining room table with my parents), I assumed that meant that we would have to buy more post cards. So, I hid my camera inside my coat and took pictures from up on top.

Later, I learned that there was a rule that if the Jordanian sentry on the other side of the border saw anything that resembled the barrel of a gun, he would be allowed to shoot. At that moment, I felt that – as in the Hebrew expression – I had a lot more luck than brains.

Years later, on my first visit to South Africa, I had a similar kind of experience. It was 1978, and a small delegation of educators was sent from Israel to run seminars for Jewish youth in South Africa. The community showed their appreciation for us by arranging a safari in the Kruger National Park. We rented a car and set out on our journey. There are signs in Kruger saying that you must not get out of your car except at the recognized rest-and-camping areas. We decided to ignore them. On one of the three days we spent traveling around in the park, which is several times bigger than the whole State of Israel, we saw a very cute group of monkeys and got out of the car to take pictures with them. An angry elephant started charging towards us. We ran back to the car and drove off. The elephant's huge foot was poised above the car and missed crushing us by a split-second. I realized at that point that not all rules are made to be broken; sometimes they reflect a lot of wisdom.

One of the most negative experiences on that initial trip to Israel in 1964 was my encounter with my paternal grandfather, who lived in Tel-Aviv. He had divorced my grandmother when my father was about ten years old, leaving her for a much younger and more stylish woman with whom he had already become involved while he and my grandmother were still married. He had come to the U.S. for a visit when I was about two, but other than that, I knew him only second-hand. He and his second wife saved about a hundred Jewish children during the War through the port in Lisbon. They later went to Guatemala and came back to Israel in 1948, where he served as the honorary consul of that Central American country. They had been issued the first two diplomatic passports of the new Jewish state. A biography of him was written years later, stressing all the charitable work he had done. But he was not charitable towards his family.

Meeting him was not pleasant. He had a long-standing dislike of my mother and her family, anything American, and the Jewish religion. I was already beginning to be interested in more traditional expressions of Judaism, and he thought that was backward. He was a modern, progressive and, therefore, thoroughly secular Zionist. All four of my grandparents were secularists to a greater or lesser degree, some having rebelled against their religious upbringing. The only one who seemed actively anti-religious was my paternal grandfather who, in his youth in Istanbul, had been a follower of Mustafa Kemal Ataturk.

He would surely have preferred a different kind of granddaughter, someone prettier and more stylish, one he could show off to his friends. I was too serious and intellectual as well as being interested in religion. He had many contacts with "important" people, including politicians, journalists, cultural icons, etc. It turns out that because I didn't come to one of his parties, I missed out on meeting Daniel Barenboim. My grandfather arranged for me to be interviewed by a reporter from *LaI-sha*, a popular women's magazine. They sent a photographer and took a lot of pictures.

I then saw the article in print. It began with three Hebrew words that mean, "She isn't pretty." I wondered why they needed to say that when there were so many pictures; the readers could have judged for themselves. The article went on to say something like, "But when she opens her mouth, you can see that she's bright and has what to say." That article did a lot of damage to my teenage psyche. Years later, after I had made *Aliyah*, I saw the piece again in a pile of old magazines, I think in a beauty salon. It didn't help my adult psyche that much, either.

I spent my "gap year" in Israel. In those days, we didn't have that concept yet. We thought we were simply taking off a year between high school and college. The program, known as the Young Judaea Year Course, included five months of Hebrew and Jewish studies in Jerusalem, one month on a moshav, three months on a kibbutz, one month of what they called Special Interest, and a two-week summary session in Haifa. Now, participants in gap year programs can usually get full college credit and finish their studies quicker. I got only language credit for the Hebrew and still did four years of college. In retrospect, I'm not sorry about that.

But my first day in Israel was a disaster. Israel in the 1960s was a far less open and pluralistic society than it became decades later. In those days, people were snubbed on the street for wearing American-style Bermuda shorts, or doing anything else that didn't quite fit in. The vast majority of the men were wearing one of two different shirts, those being the two featured that season in the now-defunct Atta department store. There were two kinds of cheese – white and yellow; two kinds of wine – sweet and sweeter. Israeli society was often depicted as primarily secular Jewish, Socialist-Zionist, *Ashkenazi*. The rest of society – Arabs, religious Jews of various kinds, other kinds of Zionists or non-Zionists, Jews from Oriental or *Sephardi* backgrounds – were all either ignored or perceived as peripheral.

On that particular day, in September of 1965, I wore Bermuda shorts and walked down Strauss Street into the center of downtown West Jerusalem. It felt like at least 200 people made a face at me, offered a nasty comment, or just frowned at my attire. I wanted nothing else than to turn around and go back to the U.S.

We were the first Year Course to come by plane; the others had cruised on a boat, beginning their Hebrew studies and getting to know each other. We were the first – and, perhaps, only – Young Judaea Year Course that had no American counselors. We had an Israeli man, who was nice enough, but we also had a South African couple and a Scottish woman who, we felt, didn't understand us at all. I broke curfew several times and got into trouble with them. I also had a lot of other personal difficulties that year. One of the difficulties was in discovering how inept I was when it came to agricultural work, ironing and various other things I had to do during the periods on the moshav and the kibbutz. A story from the kibbutz illustrates this best: seeing that I was no good at agricultural work, the kibbutz decided to use me in their communal dining room. The one thing I *was* good at was remembering which members of the kibbutz liked coffee and which liked tea; who wanted their tuna fish with mayonnaise, and who without; and that sort of thing. On Fridays they used to serve a light dairy lunch, in preparation for the big Shabbat dinner in the evening. One Friday, I was carrying into the dining room a tray with perhaps sixteen or so yogurts. I slipped, and all sixteen yogurts went flying in the air, onto the walls and the floor. Three hundred pairs of eyes looked at me and at the awful mess I had made. As traumatic experiences do, it brought me back to the many earlier embarrassments and defeats in my life.

For example, when I was in kindergarten, my parents signed me up for a class in tap dancing. After about three months, the teacher asked them to take me out of the group, saying that I was holding everybody else back. I'm sure that the fact that as an adult, one of the things I like most is folk dancing, is related to that initial sense of shame and my subsequent discovery that I'm really not so terrible at dancing. And I enjoy it.

Similarly, I don't drive. I did spend some anxious months trying to learn how to drive. When I was 18, I went for the test. All the other people being tested that day were 16. They all passed; I didn't. My hands were shaking on the wheel and I couldn't even back up the car properly. This may have been the first test I ever failed in my life, so I guess I must have been traumatized. The embarrassment has followed me ever since, and I have never learned how to drive. It is one of my regrets. Looking at my failures, I remember what Winston Churchill said, "Success is going from failure to failure without loss of enthusiasm."

But there were two major and, I believe, positive, changes in my life that were sparked by my experiences on the Year Course. The first was in the area of religion. I had been keeping a certain level of kashrut since the time I was about 13. I was thinking about becoming more traditional in my Jewish observance. Some of this was thanks to my experiences in Young Judaea, especially at camp. The first time I ever experienced a truly meaningful Shabbat, it was there.

I did many foolish things as a teenager (and maybe even more as an adult!) but one thing I am proud of is a wise decision I reached at the age of 16 or 17. I have always had many questions and doubts and I still have them. As a kid, I thought that if I remained "outside the system," all I would have would be my questions. If I chose to join "the system," I would probably still retain my questions, but I would also have a community, an identity, a sense of belonging, traditions, festivals, ideas, texts, practices and maybe even some answers. Clearly, I opted for the latter.

Early in our year in Israel, we were asked if we needed or wanted home hospitality with families for Rosh Hashanah. I indicated that I would like a "moderately traditional family." You can imagine my surprise when I arrived at the home of the family and the door was opened by man wearing a shtreimel (fur hat, worn by Hassidim). I wondered what it might have been like if I had asked for a *very* traditional family. I became friendly with this family and continued to stay in contact with them for several years. Through my friendship with them, I accumulated several "anthropological" experiences in places like B'nei Brak and K'far Habad.

That year, I also first met Michael and Geula Rosenak. I had heard of Mike – later professor of education at the Hebrew University – before that when, as a Young Judaea programmer, I read his wonderful booklets and programming guides. But we met when I came on the Year Course in 1965. Not only was Mike my teacher for modern Jewish history; when offered a choice of *chugei bayit* –classes based largely on readings and discussion on different topics, held in the homes of the teachers – I elected to take Mike's *chug* on Modern Jewish Thought. During our weekly meetings in his living room, I heard, for the first time, about Martin Buber, Franz Rosenzweig, Hermann Cohen and others. But perhaps even more significantly for my personal development, I was exposed to a modern Orthodox household in which what impressed me was the depth and breadth of the library and the music collection. I realized that one could be fully observant as a Jew as well as seriously engaged with general culture. Mike became for me a role model as well as a teacher and, years later, a colleague and friend.

Later in the year, when it came time to choose our kibbutz, we had a choice among several secular kibbutzim or a religious one. As a practical-minded almost-nineteen-year-old, I figured that by going to a religious kibbutz, I would gain two experiences for the price of one: I would see what kibbutz life was like and I would also see what being religious was like. I chose to spend three months on a religious kibbutz – Kibbutz Sh'luchot in the Bet She'An Valley, probably one of the two or three hottest places in the whole country. I was there from March to June of 1966, and there were days when the temperature reached over 40 degrees (Celsius), although it wasn't yet summer. This was before air conditioning. We had some small fans in our volunteers' quarters. We learned that if we stripped, covered ourselves with wet towels and lay in front of the fan, we could just about survive the heat.

In addition to being a very hot place, Sh'luchot in those days had the reputation of being the most liberal of all the Orthodox kibbutzim in Israel. Women who were working in the fields still wore short-shorts and when they came into the communal dining room for lunch, they did not change their attire. Our group of American teenagers worked about five-and-a-half days per week, and studied Judaism for an additional half a day. It was during my time on the kibbutz that I made a commitment to being an observant Jew. It is probably significant in my life that I made this commitment (to God and to myself) within the context of a relatively liberal and Socialist community.

The second area in which I experienced a major change was in my attitude to teaching. I hadn't liked school at all until the 5th grade, and I didn't like it a lot until college. I had some very negative educational experiences growing up. In the 4th grade, a friend of mine and I used to sit together in class and talk a lot. The teacher made us sit on opposite sides of the room. We went to the encyclopedia and learned – by ourselves – the alphabet for American Sign Language. We signed to each other, thus "talking" without making a sound. When the teacher caught us, she punished us.

Many years later, when I was training teachers, I used to offer this as an example of what not to do. In retrospect, the teacher could have used it as a teaching opportunity. The whole class could have learned signing; we could have explored disabilities, language, the meaning of "noise," the concept of communication, etc. But that would have involved some creativity. At the time, I thought that teaching was a fairly uncreative, almost "low-level" profession.

It's a bit odd that I felt that way. After all, both of my parents were trained social workers – not exactly a highly rated profession in itself. But although my family valued education highly, we tended to look down on teachers.

The first five months of my year program in Israel were spent living and studying in downtown West Jerusalem. I was in the highest level of the Ulpan, the intensive framework for learning Hebrew language and literature. I had a marvelous teacher, a young woman (I think she was 26 at the time), named Chana Gat, who had a newborn baby son. Unfortunately, she died of cancer a few decades later, in her early 50's. I really admired her, and she was a very good teacher.

Since I knew Hebrew so well, I participated once or twice a week in an important extra-curricular activity. There was a man called Yaakov Maimon who was the stenographer of the Knesset. At that time, Israel was still receiving many new immigrants each year, from far-flung parts of the world like Morocco, Yemen, Kurdistan, etc. Some of these folks were illiterate in any language; others simply did not know Hebrew. Maimon searched for anyone who knew some Hebrew and "conscripted" them to get on a truck and go with him into a neighborhood full of new immigrants. He gave us notebooks and pencils and we were supposed to teach others whatever little Hebrew we knew ourselves. He collected the notebooks at the end of each teaching session – I'm not sure he actually went over everything we had written. The purpose was to teach people how to read and write in Hebrew, and encourage conversation, using basic vocabulary. I remember that I had a particularly gratifying experience with some children who had come from India.

Years later, Maimon won the Israel Prize for his efforts. But I came away with two prizes myself. One was that I met Beth, who was a Junior Year Abroad student from Barnard, the school to which I was intending to go after that year in Israel. We met on one of these trucks going to teach new immigrants. The following year, when I was a freshman in college and she was a senior, we remained in contact. She and her British husband David came to live in Israel – Rehovot – years later and the three of us are good friends.

The second prize was a revolution in my attitude towards teaching. When the month of Special Interest came around – I think it was June to July – I realized that I had very few marketable skills. One of our group was a SCUBA diver, another was good with animals and could work at the zoo, and so on. The only thing I felt I could do was teach Hebrew. I went back to Yaakov Maimon and asked if I could work with him daily for a month. It was during that month that my attitude changed. I remember one very frustrating experience with some women from Kurdistan, who weren't literate in any language. I spent a long time trying to explain to them the connections among words, sounds and letters; I didn't succeed. But I did realize that teaching can be a true challenge to one's intellect and creativity. I became a teacher.

When I came back from the Young Judaea program to start my university studies at Barnard, I was a newly-observant modern Orthodox Jew. I still didn't quite understand all the distinctions and nuances, and I spent a great deal of time with observant Jews from the Conservative movement, at our neighboring institution, the Jewish Theological Seminary. I worked as a counselor and group leader within Young Judaea, thinking that by doing so, I was enabling other Young Judaeans to have the same kind of life-transforming experience I had just had. But for my own personal needs, I thought it might be better for me to join the religious Zionist youth movement, *B'nei Akiva*. In those days, *B'nei Akiva* was still a Socialist movement, educating its graduates to go to Israel and join (or start) a religious kibbutz. In some ways, it was a kind of religious equivalent of *Hashomer HaTzair*, which had a rival youth movement called *Mizrahi HaTzair*, less doctrinaire in its ideology, that encouraged young religious immigrants to settle in development towns and do educational and community work there. They used to have lengthy arguments about who were the true religious *halutzim*, pioneers. Since I had some thoughts about going back to live on a religious kibbutz, I started "to hang around" with a group of graduates of *B'nei Akiva*.

The problem was that they weren't at all friendly to me. Many of them had known each other since pre-school and I was definitely an outsider. After a few months, I left their group. I did try to join some groups that were forming among Young Judaea graduates. The first group re-established Moshav N'veh Ilan in the Judean hills, and the second started Kibbutz Ketura in the *Arava*. But the former were older than I and the latter, younger. So I never joined a settlement group and realized after a while that I'm a bit of an individualist for whom personal autonomy is important. I wouldn't want important decisions about my life to be made at a general meeting of the community.

By now, it was after 1967 and the Six-Day War had changed the face of Israel. The group that had not been friendly towards me became the nucleus for the American group that joined their Israeli counterparts and re-established Kibbutz K'far Etzion in the *Etzion* Bloc south of Jerusalem. I often wonder what might have happened had they been friendlier. Would I now be living in a settlement in the territories? As feminists are fond of saying, "The personal is political."

The Rest of the Family

MY GRANDPARENTS ON MY FATHER'S SIDE were Turkish Jews, but not *Sephardim*. They were Yiddish-speaking *Ashkenazim* who, a couple of generations earlier, had crossed the Black Sea from Odessa and arrived in Istanbul. My father's first language was Yiddish. His family left Istanbul for Vienna when he was three, so he didn't know much Turkish. My grandmother, Bobbie Ina, his mother, lived with us from the time I was about 2 and basically raised my sister and me while my mother was out working. She did speak Turkish, together with a smattering of other languages she picked up in the streets of the city: a little Greek, a little Armenian and a little Ladino. She attended an elementary school of the Alliance Israelite Universelle and learned French (and, later, some German). Sarina (Ina was a nickname) prepared for us certain Turkish foods – to this day, I love *borekas* – and we grew up listening to the music of this region. My father became the epitome of "the wandering Jew." Born in Istanbul, he attended elementary school in Vienna, high school in Berlin (apparently, the same school as Willy Brandt) and university in Paris.

Many years later, my sister, who had come to live in Israel before me, married a man – Ami Cohen – from Morocco. They spent about twenty-five years living on a moshav in the south. It was called *"Nir Yisrael"*; literally, "the field of Israel." Although my brother-in-law had come from quite a traditional Moroccan-Jewish family, he himself dropped almost all the religious practices with which he had grown up. He and my sister maintained a secular Israeli home. By this time, I was modern Orthodox and visiting them for Shabbat or most festivals posed a challenge – even their kitchen wasn't kosher. Thus, one of the occasions when I could easily visit them was *Tu B'Shevat*, Jewish Arbor Day, a minor festival in our winter, without restrictions on activities such as travel and without binding rituals. The custom on this day is to eat different kinds of fresh or, especially, dried fruits and to plant trees in Israel.

When I arrived on the moshav, my sister asked me to go to the community kindergarten and pick up her 5-year-old son. The word for kindergarten in Hebrew is *gan*; literally, "garden." It is the same word that is used in the Torah for the Garden of Eden. My nephew's first name is Nitzan; literally, "bud." Here I was in the field of Israel, on Arbor Day, headed for the garden, to pick up my nephew, Bud. As all the children coming out of the *gan*, Nitzan was carrying a potted plant. I am a total ignoramus when it comes to flora, so I asked him what kind of plant it was. He told me, "the wandering Jew . . ."

On one side of his family, Nitzan has roots in Poland, the U.S., Turkey, Austria, Germany and France; on the other side, Morocco. But now "the wandering Jew" was to be given a permanent home in the land of Israel.

My father used to tell a wonderful story about his doctoral thesis at the Sorbonne. As a young student, in his early 20s, he told the doctoral adviser that he wanted to write a dissertation on the process by which European women gained the right to vote, and its implications for European politics. The professor replied, "No, that's not interesting; no one cares about that." Disappointed, my father asked if the adviser had a different suggestion. The adviser said, "Well, you're from Turkey. From the 14th century, there was an elite unit in the Turkish Army called the Janissaries. No one has ever written a dissertation about them." And so my father came to write about the Janissaries. I've never read it, but two of my friends who read French easily, have. They have told me that it's interesting. On the other hand, if my father had written the first dissertation ever in gender studies, on women's suffrage . . . who knows? Perhaps we would have become affluent or, at least, famous?

After receiving his doctorate in history, my father left Europe and headed for the United States, in order to volunteer for the American Army, which sent him back overseas. He served in counter-intelligence, using his knowledge of European languages to interrogate spies. As a new recruit, before going to Europe, he met my mother in New York. She was a native of Brooklyn, the older daughter of Polish-Jewish immigrants. My favorite story from that period is that not long after they met and started going out, it was February. On Valentine's Day, my mother, or, the woman who would later become my mother, came home and found a bouquet of flowers and a box of chocolates on her kitchen table. She asked the man who was to become my father, "But, I thought you didn't believe in Valentine's Day." He answered, "I don't, but I believe in you."

They married a few weeks after Pearl Harbor and spent the first period of their married life together living on an army base in Clemson, South Carolina. That must have been very hard for the cosmopolitan European and his transplanted New Yorker wife. Then, he was sent overseas for two years. That, of course, was many decades before e-mail, cell phones and all the rest. I often wonder what it must have been like for my mother, a very young and naïve woman, to have spent all that time waiting for my father. It took about a year after the end of the War for my father to return home, but shortly afterwards, I was conceived.

I was born in New York City in 1947 on April 19th. Lately I have taken to celebrating my Hebrew birth date, which is the 29th of Nissan. April 19th turns out to have been a date with many violent historical associations: Paul Revere's famous midnight ride, signaling the beginning of the American Revolution, took place in 1775, from April 18th to the 19th, so that when we lived in Massachusetts, my birthday was a public holiday called Patriots' Day and we didn't have to go to school. The Arab uprising in Mandatory Palestine began on April 19th, 1936 and the Warsaw Ghetto revolt on April 19th, 1943. The FBI raid on the Branch Davidian ranch near Waco occurred on April 19th, 1993, and, two years later on the same date, Timothy McVeigh killed and wounded hundreds in Oklahoma City.

However, my Hebrew birth date, the 29th of Nissan, falls in between Israel's Holocaust Remembrance Day, *Yom HaShoah* – the 27th of Nissan – and Israeli Independence Day, *Yom HaAtzmaut*, the 5th of Iyyar. This is quite meaningful to me, as I was born after the Shoah and before the establishment of the State. My mother told me several times that the first day I ever stood up was November 29th, 1947, at the age of seven months and ten days – the day the United Nations

Family portrait from 1958. Top row, left to right: Sylvia and
Nahum Weissman. Middle Row, left to right: the author; paternal
grandmother, Bobbie Ina; and maternal grandmother, Bobbie
Fela. Bottom row: author's sister, Judy, holding Trusty.

voted for the partition plan to end the British Mandate and establish a
Jewish state and an Arab state. That sounds apocryphal to me, but she
insisted it was true.

My sister Judy was born three years and four months after me, in
Detroit. It was very important to our parents that we be given a solid

Author's parents, Nahum and Sylvia Weissman

Hebrew and Jewish education, albeit not a religious one. The "problem" was that, beginning in Akron, the community educational options involved attending synagogue services. I liked them, largely because of the singing. When I was about ten years old, we joined a Reform temple in Akron. My parents didn't enjoy the rather formal services very much, so they then joined a Conservative synagogue, which they liked more. I had my Bat Mitzvah there.

I recently heard a lecture by Professor Jonathan Sarna of Brandeis University, perhaps the leading expert on American Jewish history. He noted that many self-identified secular Jews began to join synagogues in the 1950s. I had always thought that it was a natural result of the general move out of major Jewish population centers into the suburbs and exurbs. After all, when you live in Brooklyn, you can absorb Jewishness on the street. But when you live in a smaller community, you may feel a need to affiliate with a synagogue, which you never felt before. I remember the general American ethos of the time: "The family that prays together stays together."

Sarna suggested that this development reflected the influence of the McCarthy era. I can remember seeing Robert Welch on television in the Army-McCarthy hearings. But I'm embarrassed to say I never really discussed the effects of that period with my parents. Sarna said that the word "secular" had become identified in the American mind with "Communist," so many secular Jews chose to join synagogues. It's an interesting idea.

When we lived in Haverhill, Massachusetts – a small town on the New Hampshire border, more than an hour north of Boston – there was only one synagogue, which my sister called "reconservadox." They used to use the old Union Prayerbook (Reform) at their late Friday evening services; a traditional Orthodox prayer book for Shabbat morning; and the Silverman (Conservative) for the High Holidays. I was one of the few who stayed in Hebrew School after my Bat Mitzvah. But rather quickly, we saw that if I wanted to continue my Jewish education in a serious way, this would not be the answer.

My parents looked around for a solution. They found a synagogue in Brookline that had a three-day-a-week program. They took me for a meeting with the principal. He decided to permit me to attend only on Sunday mornings and to make up the work for the two afternoons a week I would not be able to come. For a whole year, my father, who worked hard during the week, got up early every Sunday morning to drive me to Boston. While I was in class, he would sit and read in the library. We then had lunch at a kosher deli down the street from the synagogue and drove back home to Haverhill. I told this story once, and a friend said, "You learned a lot more than Hebrew on those Sundays." I have to say that my mother added a great deal by teaching me Hebrew grammar. Her Jewish knowledge, especially of Hebrew, was much more impressive than my father's. But they were both deeply committed to the concept.

Both Jewish and general education were highly valued in our home, as was "culture"; I learned to love music, cinema, reading, singing, largely because my parents loved them, too. They had friends of different races and backgrounds, before it became fashionable. When I was quite young, they took me with them on condolence calls, so I could learn the value of *nihum avelim*, comforting the mourners. I would say that although they did not really perform the commandments between a person and God – I sometimes joke and say that I'm a product of a mixed marriage, because my father was an atheist and my mother, an agnostic – they certainly performed many commandments between a person and his/her fellow human beings. They taught by example. My father used to have a silly remark which he said to us, "A lot of heredity comes through the genes." That is undoubtedly true, but I think that the atmosphere and environment in which one is raised are also crucial.

As I have already mentioned, both of my parents were social workers. My father became a social worker earlier, in the early 1950s. For much of his professional life, he worked in the Jewish Community Center movement. There is a great deal of mobility in that field, and that is largely responsible for the fact that I grew up in four different states – New York, Michigan, Ohio and Massachusetts. Years later, both my sister and I settled in Israel – she earlier than I – and we have sometimes discussed the advantage we had from our childhood, of being able to adapt ourselves to new places and new situations. At the time, however, we experienced the moves as difficult, if not downright traumatic. The summer I was 13, we moved from Akron to Haverhill. I broke out in eczema.

My father worked in the JCC movement in the 1950s, into the early 1960s. This was before the movement as a whole adopted informal Jewish education, and strong commitment to Jewish identity, among its goals. He was often frustrated in his work, which he felt consisted mainly of administration and neither Jewish education nor real social work. I suspect that he wasn't the easiest person to work with, either, and had great difficulty getting along with the Board members of the various communities.

My mother followed my father in going to social work school. She had worked previously in non-professional settings, but finally finished her MSW when I was in high school. One of the earlier settings was called Traveler's Aid, in Akron, Ohio. My mother worked at the central bus station, offering help to travelers who needed it. One day, around Christmas time in 1956, someone left a pregnant dog in the station. The Traveler's Aid office publicized the birth of the litter in the local newspapers. The puppies were eagerly adopted by various families; my parents decided to take home the mother dog.

The dog was a mix of terrier and chihuahua, with huge ears. We named her Trusty, for two reasons. First, my sister and I had seen the Disney film, "Lady and the Tramp," in which that is the name of one of the characters. But, secondly, I had begun my life-long obsession with programming (and I don't mean computer programming, because we hadn't yet heard of computers). I imposed on the rest of the family something I called the Weissman Family Fun Club, in which I developed and ran programs for Halloween, Washington's Birthday, and other occasions, in which they all had to take part. We made our new pet the trustee – hence, Trusty.

Fairly quickly, we learned that we liked living in Massachusetts and New England, in general, more than in Ohio and the Midwest. In Akron, I attended Simon Perkins Junior H.S. for a whole year and never found out who he was. It turns out that he was one of the founders of Akron and had served as a brigadier-general during the War of 1812. But in Haverhill, my sister and I attended the John Greenleaf Whittier Middle School and, although he may have been a second-rate poet, at least we knew his work. He is most famous for the line: "For of all sad words of tongue or pen, the saddest are these: It might have been."

1965 was the 325th anniversary of the incorporation of Haverhill as a city, and the year I graduated from Haverhill High School. One of the ways in which Haverhill celebrated its anniversary was through a performance showcasing the diverse ethnic heritage of the residents. There were presentations by Greeks and Armenians and I led and even choreographed an Israeli dance for some of the Jewish kids. As the valedictorian of my class, I gave a speech that I called, "New England: Puritan and Rebel." I guess you could say that, to this day, I identify personally with that contrast.

In most high school yearbooks, there are categories called "Most Likely to Succeed," "Miss Personality," "Mr. Athlete," and so on. In my high school yearbook, although I did graduate first in our class,

I'm not given the distinction of "Miss Student" or "Miss Brains." I'm designated as "Miss Traveler." That reflects my travels around the country to attend various Young Judaea activities, but mostly the three weeks in which I went to Israel for the World Zionist Congress. At one point, paradoxically and somewhat absurdly, there was a question as to whether I would be allowed to graduate at all, since I had missed so many days of classes!

It turns out that between 1962 and 1965, during the years I was in high school and in Young Judaea, there were two important events going on in Europe that would deeply affect my adult life, but I didn't know about them at the time. The first was the Second Vatican Council which produced the important Church document *Nostra Aetate* that profoundly changed the relationship of Christians and Jews. It revolutionized the field of inter-religious dialogue, which would later take on great significance in my own life. The other event was the Auschwitz trial which exemplified the confrontation of German society with its tragic past. That, too, was to become an important factor in my life. But more on that later . . .

Back to my parents: After my mother finished her social work degree, and especially after they moved back to New York in 1969, she ended up doing quite a bit better – professionally and financially – than my father. I don't think he was in the least bit jealous; he seemed happy and proud. And so it was quite natural that on August 25th, 1970, my mother and I (my sister was already living in Israel) joined the first feminist march up Fifth Avenue. In those days, we weren't yet using the term "feminist"; we called it "Women's Liberation." One of the cute slogans of the march was "Don't iron while the strike is hot." I remember saying something that in retrospect would turn out to have been deeply short-sighted: I said to my mother, "This is all very well and good, but there will never be female rabbis." I was so wrong. Less than two years later, the Reform movement ordained its first female rabbi and the other movements followed suit. Now, even the Modern Orthodox ordain and have women serving in rabbinical positions, although they don't always use that title. But some do, including one who sits in front of me in the synagogue.

I had my own consciousness raised a few years before, in something that feminists like to call a "click" moment. I must say that for someone who dislikes organizational politics as much as I do, I have been significantly involved in quite a few organizations. In 1963, as an about-to-be junior in high school, I got elected Vice-President of National Young Judaea. We were two juniors on the Executive Board – a young man from Connecticut and myself. Although both juniors and seniors can be on the Board, the President is almost always a senior. The following summer, when it came time to hold elections again, both of us wanted to run for President. A *shaliach* – an educational emissary – from Israel pulled me aside in an attempt to dissuade me from running. He told me that he thought it would be much better for the image of the movement if the President were to be a male. The girls could develop a crush on him, while the boys could see him as their role model. Maybe, he said, the girls could see me as a role model, but what would happen with the boys?

I decided to ignore his advice and run anyway. I won and served as the first female President of the movement in about a dozen years. Shortly thereafter, the fellow from Connecticut dropped out of the movement and wasn't heard from again, at least in Zionist circles. I subsequently moved to Israel and became a Jewish educator. Forty-four years later, I was elected to be the first Jewish woman to serve as President of the ICCJ. But by then, my parents were long gone.

My father was named Nahum, who was one of the Biblical prophets. In Israel, it's a reasonably common name. But in the U.S., he used to get letters addressed to Hahum, Hakoum and the like. He sometimes said that he experienced his name as a kind of curse. When we moved to Haverhill, he told people just to call him Nat.

My father's avocation had been the martial arts. He earned black belts in judo, jujitsu, karate and aikido. As a young man in 1935, he joined the French judo team at the Maccabiah games in Palestine. Into his fifties, he went to the dojo several times a week, working out with much younger people. I think the women in the family – my mother, my sister and I – reacted against this by becoming seriously unathletic. He was in good enough shape to survive both a heart attack, at age 57, and a stroke, at 66. There is a toy in Israel called Nahum-Takum, literally, "Nahum, get up," that you punch down, and it bounces back. I think that in English, this kind of toy would be called a "bop bag" or "punching clown." We thought of Nahum in this respect as having great resilience. He did bounce back twice, but not the third time.

After the heart attack, he stopped doing judo and looked around for something else with which to fill his time. After the Yom Kippur War in

1973, my father started thinking about doing something to help Israel. The question he asked himself was: who are the people in America most connected with Israel? The answer he gave himself to that question was, "people whose children and grand-children have made *Aliyah*." He decided to organize them into a group.

At first, my father did not envision the organization as a support group for its members. That is what it eventually became for some, but my father initially conceived of it as a pressure group within the community, that would promote the sale of Israeli products, make low-income loans available to immigrants who were buying homes in Israel, encourage its members to learn some rudimentary Hebrew so they could communicate with their grandchildren, etc. At first, my mother didn't like the idea, but she finally came around, and at one point, even served as National President.

The organization started in 1974, with a meeting of three couples in my parents' living room. What they had in common was that they all had children who had made *Aliyah*. For the first few years, my parents traveled around the U.S. and parts of Canada, usually at their own expense, helping to organize local chapters of P'NAI, the Parents of North American Israelis. The last time I was at all involved, they numbered over 7,000 members in dozens of chapters. The parents were Zionists and non-Zionists, religious and secular, even Jews and non-Jews (because some of the children who made *Aliyah* were converts to Judaism)! But they shared a common concern for their families in Israel.

When my mother was active in P'NAI, one of her duties was "the third suitcase." Now, in the 21st century, airlines rarely allow economy passengers more than one suitcase and, I understand, on many American domestic flights, you are not allowed any free baggage. But in those days, one of the perks of being a member of P'NAI was that El Al would allow you to take a third suitcase – usually full of clothes and toys for the grandchildren in Israel. P'NAI members in the tri-state Greater New York area who were planning a family visit to Israel would call our home and my mother would write down their names on a list she would then send to El Al. But, as a social worker, she turned what could have been a technical-administrative chore into an opportunity to converse with the people and find out how many children they had in Israel, where they lived, what they did, etc. It helped her to make connections among different people.

The Weissmans, at a PNAI convention in 1984, photo by Lisa Mishli

After my parents died and we had to close up their apartment in Riverdale, I collected their papers and brought them to the Central Zionist Archive in Jerusalem. The archivist was interested in them, because they had started a new "Zionist" organization. A sub-archive was set up for them.

In 1993, my father died of cancer. It came as quite a shock to the family, because we thought that he would be able to bounce back, as he had twice before. But this time, after a procedure of cauterizing the tumor, all of his body systems just broke down. He was 79. The three of us who were left – my mother, my sister and I – were sitting shiva and a colleague of my mother's came to pay her a condolence call. This particular colleague, whose name was Doris, was Jewish but, it turned out, totally ignorant of any Jewish customs. The expression *Mazel Tov* is reserved for happy occasions. It's sort of half-way between "congrat-ulations" and "good luck." When one pays a condolence call, there are traditional formulations for consolation. But the most appropriate thing to say may simply be, "I'm sorry for your loss."

Doris came all the way up to Riverdale, where we were sitting. She entered the room, went over to my mother, took her hand, and said,

"Sylvia – Mazel Tov." My mother, without skipping a beat, said, "Thank you, Doris; I know what you mean."

Less than three years after my father died, my mother was diagnosed with Stage 4 lung cancer, of the kind that non-smokers get. At first, the doctors said she had a few more years left, but that quickly changed to a few more months. I went to visit her in February of 1996, during a period of terrorist bus explosions in Jerusalem. I was with her for three weeks. I took her to her various appointments and treatments, but there seemed to be little I could do to really help.

I did make several hours of tapes, interviewing her about her life, her memories and the family stories. Some of this present memoir is based on those tapes. She seemed to enjoy the conversations, but they were tiring for her, so we did no more than 20–30 minutes a day, for several days. I'm just sorry I hadn't thought of this much earlier, and similarly interviewed my father or even my grandparents.

Both of my parents died on the 21st day of the respective Hebrew months, he in Nissan, she in Adar. Thus she died exactly two years and eleven months after him, or two years to the day that I stopped saying Kaddish for him. In Hebrew, letters have numerical value. If you turn around the letters of 21, *kaf aleph*, you get *ach*, as in the verse, (Deut. 16:15), "you shall be altogether joyful." But this phrase for "altogether joyful" can also mean "to minimize one's joy." My mother died exactly one week after Purim and my father, on the 7th day of Passover. My joy on these festivals has, ever since, been mixed with sorrow and longing.

But as a colleague once told me, "to minimize" doesn't mean "to negate completely." We can still rejoice, albeit in a more tempered way.

College and Graduate Studies

I ATTENDED BARNARD COLLEGE FROM 1966 to 1970. I had been accepted under a program called Early Decision, at the beginning of my senior year in high school and with a year's deferment to go to Israel. This meant that I never applied to any other college. Barnard was definitely the right school for me. I still have a few close friends whom I met there, as well as very fond memories and I think some serious intellectual and cultural baggage. During that period, I was on campus for only six semesters, two of which were disrupted by demonstrations. This is also because I spent my Junior Year Abroad, at the Hebrew University in Jerusalem. The only college year that I was at Barnard and that began and ended as planned, without political turmoil in New York, was my freshman year, 1966–67. Clearly, there was political turmoil that year in the Middle East, especially in June of 1967.

Perhaps strangely, the Six-Day War didn't affect my Zionist commitment as much as it did some people's. (The Yom Kippur War, for example, precipitated my becoming an Israeli citizen.) I spent one day of the War trying to raise money for Israel – I collected something like $32! – and another two days packing medicines to send to the Hadassah Hospital. Not very impressive for someone who was serving at the time as Israel Chair of the American Jewish Youth Council.

I remember that in the early summer, just after the end of the fighting, the Young Judaea leaders who would be working in our national camp met to discuss how the War would affect us. Some of the more "radical" in our group thought we should go to Israel to help. We debated back and forth.

I later learned that that evening, the entire national leadership of the *Beitar* youth movement – the right-wing Zionists associated with Jabotinsky and, later, Begin – boarded a plane and left for Israel. At the time, I admired their commitment. In retrospect, I'm wary of it. Perhaps it's that old Young Judaea "wishy-washy" mistrust of collectivist thinking and ideological rigidity. On the far left, *or* the far right.

For much of my freshman year at Barnard, I participated in something called HEP – the Harlem Education Program. I tutored a 9-year-old girl in Harlem. In addition to having what I unprofessionally diagnosed as mild retardation, she was certainly what we used to call "culturally deprived." I was supposed to help her with homework and reading. I thought we could do it in her home, but there was only one chair, in great need of repair, and often, no light bulb. I made the decision in good weather to work outside, in the park, and in inclement weather, at the local bowling alley. True, it was very noisy, but at least it was well-lit and the seats were comfortable. One evening towards the end of the school year, I brought her to Barnard for dinner and a visit to our library. There was a music corner in the library and she seemed to enjoy listening to records through the earphones.

This was a real eye-opener for me. Although my family never seemed to have enough money, we were definitely in the upper middle class educationally and professionally. I had never really been exposed to poverty. This experience prepared me somewhat for my first full-time job after college (1970–71) as an employment counselor in the South Bronx.

Getting back to college itself: I was on campus for the spring demonstrations in 1968 and 1970. Both of these involved a combination of issues. We were protesting Columbia University's complicity with the Vietnam War, but also its behavior as a landlord in neighboring Harlem.

One of my close friends in college was a Unitarian named Anne. Many Unitarians were formerly Jews; Anne's family had been Presbyterian. We stayed in contact on and off for years. We usually agreed on political, social and cultural issues. But during the student strike in 1968, we had a disagreement that taught me something about a possible difference between Jewish and other values.

Classes had been disrupted for several weeks. In retrospect, it seemed to me that some of the most interesting courses I had in college were curtailed by one revolution or another. I was hoping that we would be able to go back to class and finish the semester. Anne said that we had been out of the framework for so long, we were probably no longer in the mood or the mind-set to go back. I said, "If we go back, it will put us in the mind-set."

I may not have realized it at the time, but that is an echo of *Sefer HaHinukh*, literally, the Book of Education, from 13th century Spain. The book lists and elaborates in order all the 613 commandments that appear in the Torah and comments on them. In what is undoubtedly one of the best-known passages in the medieval book, the commentator, discussing the somewhat obscure prohibition against breaking the bones of the Paschal lamb (in Exodus 12:46), says, "The hearts are drawn to the activities." In other words, you don't wait until you're in the mood to do something; you do it and that puts you in the right mood.

But we didn't go back to classes. Some of the professors, in sympathy with the striking students, held classes outside the buildings, on the lawn, although the topics of the classes reflected the strike and not the original themes of the courses. I became aware for the first time of the diversity of political and ideological subgroups on the Columbia-Barnard campus. I hadn't really known before about the Maoists and the Trotskyites. They were generally humorless people who objected to those who were organizing "TGIF – Thank God it's Friday" parties during the strike, with ice cream, balloons and rock music. When a Maoist or a Trotskyite told someone, "We're making a revolution; we don't have time for this," he was told, "I don't support the revolution if I can't have ice cream and music." At that point, I realized that since I began observing the Shabbat two years earlier, I had been celebrating a kind of weekly TGIF.

Groups such as SDS – Students for a Democratic Society – occupied several of the buildings on the Columbia campus. I knew two observant Jewish men who were sitting in the buildings, but who left Friday afternoon, to buy provisions for Shabbat. They have both since come to live in Israel, and all three of us live in the southeastern corner of West Jerusalem. There were many groups among the students, and each had its own colored armband. There was one shade for people who totally identified with the strike; another for those who identified with

Purim costume: "Reality is complex"

the goals, but not the means. There was one for people less confident ideologically, but who opposed violence on both sides. I chose to wear an armband that projected the message, "I'm a bit confused, but I'm willing to help if there's a possibility that anyone will be hurt." The truth is that my views are generally too complicated to be summarized by one armband or lapel pin. In fact, one year, I came dressed for Purim as ½ devil, ½ angel, with a sign reading: "Reality is complex."

During that period, I became the first person in my family – on both sides, for several generations – to cross a picket line. Being Socialists or Social Democrats, my family always identified with the workers, not the owners. I remember as a child being taken to Rockefeller Center by my maternal grandmother, Bobbie Fela. We were supposed to go to the Radio City Music Hall. But we saw that the Rockettes were on strike and we turned around and left. Therefore, it was with some trepidation that I did cross a picket line in 1968, to go into the college library. In my mind at the time, there were two voices: one echoed my grandmother, saying, "We don't cross a picket line"; the other said, "We can't be prevented from reading books."

During my Junior Year, 1968–69, I went to Israel to study on the One-Year Program for Overseas Students at the Hebrew University. That year, I also served as counselor for the Young Judaea Year Course, one of whose participants happened to have been my sister. In retrospect, she informed me that it was nice having her sister around for the year, but that she missed having a real counselor. (Of course, on other occasions, even much more recently, she has let me know she feels that I'm acting too much as her counselor. I suppose in these situations, you can't really win.)

The first Shabbat in Jerusalem, a policeman knocked on the door of the Year Course building. In 1968, many of my contemporaries called law enforcement officers "fuzz," "pigs" and worse. This one came in to the dining room, where we were gathered for Shabbat dinner. Having experienced first-hand the spring riots on the Columbia campus and having watched on TV the Democratic convention in Chicago that summer, I was prepared for the worst. Were we making too much noise? Was he worried about drugs? Did the sight of so many hirsute and even hippy-looking young Americans arouse his suspicion?

The policeman said, "I saw that you're a new group. I just wanted to say welcome and wish you Shabbat Shalom."

The times were, as magazine articles say, "heady." We protested against the War in Vietnam, for civil rights in America, for freedom for Soviet Jews. These were the early days of the women's movement – and Barnard students had ringside seats. Just as an example of rapid social change, my freshman year, we could have men in our dorm rooms only on Sunday afternoons between 1 p.m. and 6 p.m. The rules changed for my sophomore year – now, we could have men in our rooms weekend nights until midnight. I was, as I have said, away for my junior year. When I came back for my senior year, we had co-ed dorms!

A whole generation later, in 1997, there was a group of Orthodox students at Yale, the so-called "Yale Five." They petitioned the courts to be exempt from on-campus housing. I personally thought that their requests – or, perhaps, demands – for practical arrangements that would enable them to maintain their Orthodox life style – were legitimate. What struck me as illegitimate was when some of them began to request curricular exemptions, so that they wouldn't have to read material that was challenging to their beliefs. Then why attend university at all, or at least a first-rate university like Yale?

When I returned after my Junior Year in Israel, I decided that since Israel would undoubtedly figure prominently in my future, it was high time to get to know better the land of my birth. In those days, the Greyhound Bus company had a deal where, for just $99 – don't forget this was a long time ago – you could travel all over the U.S., provided it took no more than one month. I planned a trip that took me to a boyfriend's parents in Pennsylvania, New Orleans, Houston, Albuquerque, the Grand Canyon, Los Angeles (including Disneyland), and San Francisco-Oakland-Berkeley. But I didn't budget well, neither the time nor the money, and I ended up in San Francisco, with just four days left to get back to New York, and only a few dollars in my wallet. The people with whom I was staying packed me some kosher sandwiches for the trip, but I finished them fairly quickly.

I learned the hard way that the middle of the U.S. is primarily corn fields. Because I found the scenery truly boring, and I had run out of reading material, I spent most of my last money on a crossword puzzle book to help pass the time. By the time we arrived in Philadelphia, the last stop before New York, I had a dime left in my pocket. In those days, you could still place a telephone call with a dime. My parents were supposed to come to Port Authority in Manhattan, meet me, and take me home with them for dinner. In case they weren't there, I had the dime to call them. So I couldn't use it up to buy anything else.

I was very hungry. A lady got on in Philadelphia and sat down next to me. She pulled out a beautiful bunch of grapes and asked me if I would like one. Would I? That grape was the best thing I've ever eaten. I was overcome with gratitude. I began to think about what it means to be indigent, not to know where your next meal is coming from, to be truly starving. Not an experience middle-class people often have.

As you can most likely guess, my parents met me at the bus station. I saved the dime, but I learned some lessons. For example, in the future, try to budget better – food, money and time.

During my last year of college, I lived in a suite in one of the Barnard

residences with four other young women, one of whom was my friend
Anne. In typical Barnard fashion, we were from a variety of backgrounds,
religiously and ethnically. Our dinners were a model of pluralism – some
Jews who keep kosher and some who don't; Christians; vegetarians, etc.
But all sitting at the same table and sharing whatever food we could.

Anne and I joined the many students and others from throughout the
country who descended upon Washington, D.C. in November, 1969, for
the Moratorium against the Vietnam War. Press reports said we were
up to a million. The march was to be held on Shabbat afternoon. There
were at least two busloads from New York of people who kept Shabbat
and therefore had to arrive on Friday before sundown. We brought
sleeping bags and slept on the floor of the B'nai Brith building. There,
we held our services and our Shabbat meals. It was a very meaningful
Shabbat – although the weather was freezing. The theme song of the
march was the Beatles' "All we are saying, is 'give peace a chance.'"
After the march, the people who were keeping Shabbat came back to the
building where we had been staying, for the third meal of the Shabbat,
Seudah Shlishit. Rabbi Yitz Greenberg, whom I mentioned at the very
beginning of my memoir, was with us. I will never forget what he said.
He told us that marching against the war, as we had done, was fulfilling
the true spirit of Shabbat . . . At our Barnard graduation ceremony in
1970, many of us wore black armbands on our academic robes to protest
the U.S. bombing of Cambodia and the Kent State shooting.

For several months of our senior year, the women in our suite maintained a kind of chart with our plans and prospects for the future. On
one side were our five names. On the other, categories such as "full-time
work," graduate school," "becoming a flight attendant" (known in those
days as a stewardess), etc. We charted our progress up and down with
regard to these possibilities. I learned to my dismay that I was too short
to qualify as a stewardess. But the truth is, I have since been on hundreds
of flights, but am not particularly fond of airports.

When I first applied to Barnard, I thought I might major in English
or political science. An anthropology course my freshman year made
me decide to go into that field; I still see anthropology as the "queen"
of the social sciences. We declared our majors towards the end of our
sophomore year. As there was not yet an anthropology department at
the Hebrew University, the Barnard department, in which coincidentally
most of the faculty were Jews, told me I couldn't major in anthropology

and still spend my Junior Year in Jerusalem. I quickly switched into sociology, which did exist at the Hebrew University, and was considered acceptable by international academic standards.

I met two very special teachers during my Junior Year at the Hebrew University. One was Prof. Nechama Leibowitz. If Rabbi Shlomo Carlebach revolutionized the way Jews prayed in the 20th century, Nechama revolutionized the way Jews learned Bible. I took a course with her on the stories of Abraham. Most of the other students in the class were day school graduates; I was not. They had a stronger background in Jewish texts than I did. On the first day of the class, Nechama said that anyone who couldn't read "Rashi script" shouldn't come back the following week.

Rashi, the great medieval Bible and Talmud commentator, wrote in a special script that is used for many of our classic Jewish texts. For someone who reads Hebrew, it isn't all that difficult to master, but it does involve some work. Without it, I would say the individual can be considered a functional illiterate, Jewishly. I didn't know the special script, but I learned it over that weekend and stayed in the class. When I came to live in Israel, I continued my relationship with Nechama and her extended family.

The other significant teacher I met that year was Professor Jacob Katz, founder of the discipline of modern Jewish social history. I took a course with him on the sociology of traditional Jewish society. The teaching assistant for the course went on to become an important professor in his own right, Menachem Friedman, but at the time he was a graduate student who used to ride around on a motorcycle. He later was one of the readers for my doctoral dissertation.

During that Junior Year Abroad, I spent a Shabbat visiting a family in B'nai Brak, who were associated with the great *Ponevez Yeshiva*. They were very warm and hospitable and had a wonderful sense of humor. During the Shabbat with them, I saw a huge institution in their city called *Or HaChayim*. It was a boarding school for *Sephardi* girls to be educated in the *Ashkenazi Haredi* tradition. It struck me that this would be an interesting topic for a thesis in sociology, dealing with the clash of cultures. Little did I know that in the 1980s, with the founding of the Shas party, the encounter of *Sephardim* with *Haredi* culture would become one of Israel's hottest political issues.

It was through Jacob Katz that I first heard about Sarah Schenirer and the founding of the *Bet Yaakov* movement in Poland in 1917. I eventually wrote my master's thesis in sociology on this topic, at NYU. The title was, "*Bais Yaakov*, A Women's Educational Movement in the Polish Jewish Community: A Case Study in Tradition and Modernity." (The discrepancy in the transliteration of the movement's name lies in the difference between Hebrew and Yiddish.) I have published a few articles based on my thesis and they – or the thesis itself – are cited in other works on the *Haredi* community or on women's education. I suppose you could say that one of the major themes of my life, both academically and existentially, is the potentially fruitful encounter – a process and not an event – between traditions and modernity.

Part of my graduate study was paid for by the State of New York. After graduating from college, I got a job as an employment counselor in the South Bronx. I was working in a program to get people off welfare and into the labor force. The program was sponsored by the N.Y. State Department of Labor, Division of Employment. The job was fairly low-paying and bureaucratic, but it carried with it an attractive perk – they would pay for part of my graduate study in sociology, especially if I took courses relevant to the work, such as Sociology of Occupations. I stayed only one year in that position, because the bureaucracy really got to me.

The work day was defined as 8:45 a.m. to 5 p.m. If we arrived up to 5 minutes late in the morning, the supervisor might frown, but no more than that. If we arrived ten minutes late, he would call the subway authorities to check if there had, in fact, been a delay, as we claimed. If there hadn't, we would get docked. We had two fifteen-minute coffee breaks, one in the morning and one in the afternoon, with a 45-minute lunch break. These were to be strictly adhered to. I once got into trouble with the other employees, when I decided to work through my coffee break.

On another occasion, at about 3:00 in the afternoon, I had finished all my work and literally had nothing left to do. I started to read a newspaper. The supervisor came over and said that this looked bad for the clients. I put the newspaper away and started writing a letter to my grandmother, Bobbie Fela. At that moment, I made a promise to myself: I would never again get stuck in a strict 9-to-5 job. If I have work, I can work through the night. But if I don't, I should be in charge of my own time. Especially with my work in informal education, this hasn't been a problem for me. For most of my life, I have cherished variety and have disliked routine; only in my retirement years have I more or less settled into a daily schedule. Although no two days are the same.

Part of the work itself, though, was fascinating. I interviewed many people, mostly young women, who had life experiences I had encountered only in films, such as incest and rape. It was satisfying to be able to help people build up their self-esteem and begin to develop effective work habits. I met some other counselors who became friends of mine – one whom I stayed in contact with for decades. We used to go out most days for lunch, although we couldn't exactly linger over the meal. I remember going out with them to all sorts of Chinese or Cuban restaurants in the neighborhood, where I would always have a fresh vegetable or fruit salad and a cocktail.

Being an observant Jew in that job wasn't easy. There were a number of Jews in the office, including one who had a very recognizably Jewish name but who came in to work on Yom Kippur. I used up vacation days and "Personal Days" for Jewish festivals. But, then, I had a problem in the winter: If Shabbat came in at, say, 4 p.m., I would have to leave the office by 3 in order to get home and light candles. (I would have had to finish all my Shabbat preparations the night before.) How to make up for the time I had to take off? The supervisor suggested that I work though the lunch breaks. A revolutionary idea in that office. I did it, of course, but it made moving to Israel that much more attractive, since in Israel, in those days, everyone ended their work early on Fridays, and by now, many people don't work at all on Fridays and have a 2-day weekend.

The other thing about that job is that there was one other observant Jew in the office, but in a different department. What I remember about him is his name, Mr. Reit. But he clearly wasn't – I'm pretty sure he was married and we never really had a whole conversation.

I became friends that year with another employment counselor, of Italian-American extraction. Once, I invited her for dinner (atypically, not on Shabbat – I think it may have been on a Sunday evening). I decided to serve spaghetti and meat balls, with garlic bread and wine. I think it didn't turn out so well, because my guest said, "I just *love* Jewish cooking."

The school year of 1971–72, I worked at several other, part-time jobs, and finished the course work for my master's degree. I pored over Yiddish microfilms in the YIVO library in New York, developing the basis for my thesis on *Bais Yaakov*, although I didn't finish writing it until 1977.

In the spring, I had a disappointing romance with the teaching assistant in my statistics course. I owe to him the fact that I passed the course and got my degree, but mainly, that I came to live in Israel. If he hadn't rejected me, I might have stayed in New York.

In the USSR

ONE OF THE IMPORTANT EXPERIENCES of my young adult-hood – an experience which I shared with several hundred or perhaps even several thousand other Jews in the West – was a secret trip to the Soviet Union. I went in 1971, when I was 24, for a two-week trip over Pesach, mainly to Georgia. After the War in 1967, the Soviet Union had broken its diplomatic ties with Israel. Beginning in 1968, until the fall of the USSR, the Israeli govern-ment used Zionist Jews from Western countries who could enter the Soviet Union on their passports, for various kinds of missions. In some cases, people were to make contact with Soviet Jews and smuggle in contraband items, such as Jewish ritual objects; we were also to take out names and addresses of Jews who wanted to apply for visas to Israel; later (i.e., after my time) the trip often involved teaching, performing, lecturing within Jewish communities.

The recruitment for these missions was by word of mouth. My college roommate, who had been active in *B'nei Akiva*, asked if I was interested. Through me, the "movement" spread throughout the graduates of Young Judaea. I then recommended some friends from Camp Ramah, the educational summer camp of the Conservative movement, and it spread through their circles. And so on.

I went with someone called Elliott Birnbaum z" l, who had been one of my *madrichim* and thus was perhaps 2–3 years older than I. One of his younger sisters had been on Year Course with me. The youngest in the family many years later married my Army friend. So we had quite a few personal and movement connections. The idea was that young Jews would go in pairs, often posing as couples, to various Jewish communities behind the Iron Curtain. You chose someone whom you could trust implicitly, as the trip had its dangerous elements.

I have always been fascinated – in films and books – by the theme of trust and its betrayal. I love the twists of mystery plots in which people whom you have trusted all along turn out to be the villain or the villain's accomplice. I know someone who is the child of Holocaust survivors. Her parents were hidden – I believe in the Netherlands – during the War, and within their family, the standard of judgment for people's character was, "Would you trust them to rescue us and not turn us in?"

In the late 60s, 70s, and 80s, our standard for trust became, "Is this someone with whom you could go to the Soviet Union on a secret mission?" You might think that because we all had foreign passports – American, Canadian, Swedish, French, and so on – the trips weren't particularly dangerous, because we could always ask our embassies in Russia for asylum. What was dangerous about these missions was that while we were out for the day, the hotel authorities – cooperating with the KGB – could, for example, plant a cache of drugs in our suitcases. Some of us were detained for interrogation, some were stalked, some were even "roughed up." I believe that in a few cases, our counterparts were denied entry into the USSR and sent home. We were told that in the hotel, the rooms were probably all bugged, so we should communicate important things only by using a toy called the "Magic Slate," which probably doesn't exist anymore.

We needed a cover story; in the case of Elliott and me, we had a good one. We were being sent primarily to Georgia – Tbilisi and Sukhumi – after a few days of sight-seeing in Moscow. Elliott at the time was a graduate student in botany, working on tobacco plants. Georgia was at the time the center of the Soviet tobacco industry. We made an appointment at the University there, for him to visit the botany lab and consult with colleagues. I was a graduate student in sociology; I made an appointment at the sociology department of the university. My meeting there led to a paper I wrote for one of my classes when I got back to New York.

We were supposed to pretend that we were a couple. So when I went to the travel agency, they were a bit surprised that I ordered two hotel rooms in each of the three cities we would be in. I explained that our parents were helping to pay for the trip, and they insisted that we stay in separate rooms. (This actually may have aroused the suspicion of the Soviet officials.) Of course, that was all a lie. The trip was being paid for by the Israeli government, or so I thought at the time; it was only in 2014 that I learned it was really funded by the Joint Distribution Committee – and our parents barely knew what we would be doing. I didn't tell anyone about it, other than my parents, until we returned.

We were going for two main purposes. The first was to "smuggle in" various books and items of Judaica. The second was to "smuggle out" names and addresses of Jews who wanted to make *Aliyah* and were requesting visas from the State of Israel. It was only a few years later that many Soviet Jews started to use the Israeli exit visas to get out of the USSR, but then immigrated to the US or other Diaspora countries. One of the things I smuggled in to the country was a Jewish calendar in Russian. I sewed a secret pocket inside my overcoat. This is noteworthy in itself, because I don't sew. We were just lucky that they didn't frisk us at the Moscow Airport.

Years later, when I started teaching classes in Israel about the Jewish calendar, I mentioned that smuggling is usually associated with drugs, diamonds and ammunition. I then said that from a Marxist point of view, if religion is "the opiate" of the masses, the calendar could be considered as a kind of drug. We Jews might consider it a diamond, but it can also be seen as ammunition in the struggle for Jewish identity.

There were some aspects of Soviet life and culture that were appealing. One of the things that struck me about the USSR was seeing children collect chess cards (like baseball cards) with pictures of champs on them. The look of the Soviet cities was very clean, but behind the façade of impressive architecture were serious shortages. The tourist hotel in which we stayed in Moscow, for example, had a band playing in the dining room at breakfast. Yet they ran out of coffee and butter.

Elliott and I were in the Soviet Union for two weeks, including the eight days of Passover. We would be going to the synagogue to make contact with Jews, but we weren't sure they would have Matzot or invite us home, so we brought many of the provisions with us. It is customary to eat a hard-boiled egg at the Seder. The afternoon before the first Seder, I somehow managed to get a Soviet Army officer to accompany me to a market where I bought eggs. Since I keep kosher, I told the Soviets I was a vegetarian, something that was very rare in their country. During the time we were in the Soviet Union, I ended up eating thirty-two hard-boiled eggs.

That night, we went to the synagogue in Tbilisi. The first surprise was that quite a few people asked us if we needed Matzot. For years, there had been a campaign in the West to make sure that Soviet Jews could have access to Matzot, necessary for observing Pesach. It turned out that Georgia was an exception; they baked their own Matzot all along. The second was a family that invited us for both nights of Seder, both of which ended with the singing of "*HaTikvah*," the Israeli – and to some extent, Jewish – national anthem. Its name means "The Hope."

The first night of Pesach, only the family which invited us and their two children were at the Seder. The second night, word got out that they had American Jews visiting them, and almost fifty more people showed up. A few of them were able to communicate in English; one had studied Hebrew, and had actually been arrested for doing so. When, at the end of the Seder, we sang, "Next year in Jerusalem," it had special meaning for both them and us.

I had an experience in the synagogue which I used for many years in my teaching. As I mentioned earlier, every Hebrew letter has a numerical value. Jewish mystics compute the numerical values of various words and sentences – I do, too, but for me, not a mystic, it's more of a Jewish cultural game. The traditional prayer for the local non-Jewish government is recited in Diaspora communities every Sabbath and festival. In the prayer book I found in Soviet-era Georgia, a prayer was included for the USSR. If you add up the value of the Hebrew letters for USSR, you get 380, which equals the value of the Hebrew word for Egypt. Thus, the great liberation from Egypt of our generation could be the exodus of the Soviet Jews.

We had a more difficult time in Sukhumi. The "operatives" who had sent us had given us an incorrect address for the synagogue. Friday night was to be the seventh night of Pesach, so that the eighth day of our festival would coincide with Easter. Elliott and I spent the whole of Thursday wandering around in the rain and mud, looking – in vain – for the synagogue. We came back to the hotel that evening with a deep sense of defeat.

But, then, I had an idea. One of my favorite pieces of music is the "Russian Easter Overture" by Rimsky-Korsakov. On Friday morning, I told that – it was true – to our Intourist guide and requested that we spend some time in a Russian Orthodox church that day (Good Friday). She complied with our request and we spent quite a while in the church. Finally, we told her that we had had enough. On our way out of the church, we asked her if there were any other houses of worship in the area. She pointed us in the direction of a mosque, and a synagogue. When she asked us if we wanted to visit them, we replied that we weren't all that interested but just wanted to know if they existed.

Of course, that evening, we went back and found the synagogue. In our subsequent report to the Israeli government, we corrected the mistaken address that they had. It was a great relief for us to leave the USSR. A most powerful memory for me was the contrast between entering the airport in Moscow and the one in New York. Entering the airport in Moscow, I had with me – as an MA student – some sociology books, by the likes of Peter Berger and Harvey Cox. They were duly and suspiciously scrutinized by the airport authorities. But when I came back to the U.S., I had with me almost a whole suitcase-full of Communist propaganda that I needed for the paper I was writing. The U.S. airport officials saw that I had brought in papers and books, and didn't even look to see what they were; they were searching for drugs.

Both Elliott and I came to live in Israel during the 1970s. With a Ph.D. in botany, he became a researcher at the Negev Institute. Unfortunately, in his late 50s, he died of cancer. *Y'hi zikhro barukh.* May his memory be blessed.

I don't know if Elliott ever stayed in touch with any of the people we met in the USSR who then came on *Aliyah*; I didn't. But for a brief time, I did have one family of Soviet Jewish émigrés with whom I was friends, in Jerusalem. They were a family of musicians from Moscow – father, mother and twin sons. I remember that in 1990, their first year out, we attended the same Seder in Jerusalem. They didn't know any of the songs, but we knew some Russian songs. This may have been the only Seder in my life that featured the singing – in harmony – of "The Volga Boatman." About half-way through the evening, the father said, "You know, I feel as though I have come out of Egypt." Since the *Haggadah* states, "It is incumbent on all of us to feel as though we personally left Egypt," we found this Seder particularly meaningful for us all.

The mother enrolled in a social work program at the Hebrew University, which necessitated her acquiring two new languages – Hebrew and English. She used her training to work with émigré teenagers who were having difficulties adjusting to a new and very different environment. She did so well, in both her studies and her work, that she received a special prize from the Speaker of the Knesset. I went for the ceremony. Her husband found work in music and the two boys studied at our major conservatory.

As the years went by, the boys realized that they had far greater professional opportunities for themselves in the U.S. One by one, they moved to Chicago, found work and started families. They did marry Jewish women and are raising their children with a sense of Jewish identity. Eventually, the distance from children and grandchildren was too great for the grandparents to endure, and they moved to Chicago, as well. The father plays the organ in a Reform temple. At least in that way he has a connection with the Jewish community, with the Sabbath and the festivals. I have seen them twice, on visits to Chicago.

As a student of modern Jewish history, I think that they have experienced personally the three great movements or, should I say, experiments, in 20th century Jewish life: (1) Communism; (2) Zionism; and (3) the American Diaspora experience. Their loss to Israel makes me sad.

Quiz Shows

PRIOR TO THE DAYS of so-called "reality TV" – an oxymoron if I've ever heard one – there used to be quiz shows that tested people's knowledge, without too many gimmicks. We did find out later that some of them were rigged, but not the ones I personally experienced.

Going back to the days of the Weissman Family Fun Club, I have enjoyed quizzes and other intellectual games. I inherited from my mother a love for crossword puzzles. She used to do the NY Times puzzle every day; I'm not as talented as she was in this area, and I never even bother with the Friday and Saturday puzzles, because they're too hard. In my sophomore year of college, the autumn of 1967, I tried out for the Barnard team that would appear on the General Electric College Bowl program. Not only did I make the team, I was chosen to be its captain.

We won five times in a row and retired as undefeated champions. Our first game was the fifth for the Bryn Mawr team. They were especially upset to be defeated by us. I had a strange relationship with the questions of Jewish content. Anyone who still remembers the GE College Bowl remembers that it wasn't just a question of knowing information, but also of being able to retrieve it quickly. It happened to me once or twice that the MC would start asking a question about the Bible or something else related to Judaism, and instead of immediately placing my finger on the buzzer, I would have a thought like, "Oh, this is my area; I will know the answer." But by then, it was too late, and the other team got it.

The programs were broadcast live right after the end of Shabbat. In order to be at the studio in time, I had to go to a hotel near the studio and spend Shabbat there. I remember I used to eat my Friday evening meals at a now-defunct restaurant in the area, called Gluckstern's. Bobbie Fela would come in from Jackson Heights in Queens to have dinner with me.

That year, I taught Sunday school. Once, after badly messing up on a biblical question – I can't remember if the correct answer was Solomon, and I said David, or the opposite – one of my seven-year-old pupils, obviously perturbed, asked me in a whining voice, "*G'veret* (Ms.) Weissman, how can you be our teacher, when you don't know anything yourself?"

Still, we ended up doing rather well. As captain, my job was to promote teamwork and, in case of a disagreement among the four team members as to what the correct answer was, make the binding decision. I had to learn to trust my own judgment.

After I made *Aliyah*, I looked for various ways to increase my modest income. I decided to go back to New York one summer and try to appear on a TV quiz show. (I had appeared on an Israeli quiz show and done reasonably well.) I appeared on a now long-defunct program called "The Who? What? Where? Game." The premise was that a category would pop up and the contestant had to choose a question from one of the three options. I was on a winning streak, having won two programs in a row. On my third attempt, the category that came up was "Great Comebacks." I went through the following thought process – I don't know that much about geography; perhaps I'll stick with history, and choose the Who question. The question was something about a hockey player who made a comeback and the correct answer was Bobby Orr. At the time, I didn't know the name of a single hockey star. The contestant sitting next to me chose the Where question, which was "In what Middle Eastern city is the Church of the Holy Sepulchre being restored?" The answer, of course, was Jerusalem.

I kicked myself under the table and went home with a few thousand dollars.

The 1970s

CHARLES DICKENS MIGHT HAVE characterized the 1970s in Israel as both the best of times and the worst of times. In 1972, there were two major terror incidents: the May mass shooting at the airport, and the murder of our Olympic athletes in Munich, in early September. Less than three weeks later, I arrived in Israel.

When I came to live in Jerusalem, I shared an apartment with a friend who had arrived before me. I already had several jobs set up, in informal education. One of them was teaching at the Jewish Agency Institute for Training Youth Leaders from Abroad. The Institute was housed in Jerusalem and brought together many young people, mostly aged 17–19, from different Diaspora countries, for a year of study, work and travel in Israel. They were then expected to go back to their home countries for at least two years, to be leaders of Jewish youth movements and organizations. I started working there in 1972, and a year later, the Yom Kippur War broke out. The War was a particularly difficult and frightening time for us. I was a unit head at the Institute. One night, a young woman from Britain came to see me. She was crying and saying, "Please help me – I can't pray; I wish I could pray." Without much thinking, I said to her, "You already are praying!"

At the time, the Institute, or *Machon*, was located on a campus called Kiryat Moriah, in the southern part of Jerusalem. Its educational director was my former teacher Mike Rosenak. One evening, during the most challenging days of the War, Mike spoke with the students and staff. We were sitting in the dark, because there was a blackout imposed by the

Army. He told us the story of a relative of his, Dr. Azriel Carlebach, a prominent Israeli journalist who lived during the period just before and just after the establishment of the State. Carlebach founded what was once one of our two major daily newspapers – *Ma'ariv*.

Author as a new immigrant to Israel in 1972

The *Yishuv*, or Jewish community in Palestine before the State, lost about one per cent of its population during Israel's War of Independence – 6,000 out of 600,000. That is a very high percentage. Everyone knew someone who had been killed. But, said Carlebach, 6,000 is less than the number of Jews killed *in one day* in the gas chambers and ovens of Auschwitz.

If Mike had just left the story there, without adding a positive vision for the attainment of peace, I believe it would not have been as effective in the long run. In order to mobilize the necessary sources of emotional and spiritual strength to cope with adversity, we also need more positive ideals, values, goals, which he added. I think this might have been the only time I heard Mike invoke the memory of the Holocaust to justify the continued commitment to the State of Israel. But it was a powerful message. And more than four decades later, it continues to inspire me.

Since then, I have lived through at least three more recognized wars (1982–2000 in Lebanon, 1991 in the Gulf, 2006 in Lebanon) but many more military operations, especially in Gaza. As an Israeli, I'm embarrassed to admit that sometimes our government calls a military campaign "an operation" rather than a war, so that it need not pay the compensation to Israelis required in a war. This was certainly the case in "Protective Edge" in 2014.

The whole year of the Yom Kippur War (1973–74) was difficult and depressing in Israel, especially for young single women. Three thousand men had been killed, many thousands more injured, and most of the other men were still mobilized until the spring. But, in the aftermath of the Yom Kippur War, the years I spent working at the *Machon* were relatively quieter. We even made peace with Egypt. One of the best years I remember was 1978–1979. Israel won the Eurovision Song contest – largely unknown in the U.S. – two years in a row, the second time with the remarkably upbeat song called "Hallelujah." Sadat's 1977 visit to Jerusalem began a peace process that culminated in the signing of a treaty between Israel and Egypt in 1979.

In 1978, politician and writer Yitzhak Navon was elected fifth president of the State of Israel. He was the first president with small children to move into *Beit Hanassi*, the presidential residence in Jerusalem. The festivities surrounding his inauguration, featuring his popular wife, Ophira, were capped by a musical rendition of a poem he had written, "May Great Peace Blossom in My Land." Those were hopeful days.

I enjoyed my work with Diaspora youth from all over the world. Although I worked primarily with those from English-speaking backgrounds – from the U.S., Canada, UK, Australia, New Zealand and South Africa – I also occasionally taught some of the Latin Americans, in Hebrew. One of the most wicked things I have ever done was on a *tiyul* – an excursion/hike – that took us through the Jordan Valley, when it was very hot and dry. There was one bus full of English speakers and one full of Spanish speakers. In a friendly rivalry, the kids on the two buses started pouring water at each other, through the windows of the bus, when we were driving close enough to each other to make sure that at least some of the liquid would reach its intended destination. I then hit upon the nefarious idea of pouring orange juice, which would be sticky and less pleasant than water!

After four years of living in Israel, I came back to New York for the year of 1976–77. The main reason was to enable me to finish my master's degree in sociology at NYU. I also served that year as Program Director of National Young Judaea. In that capacity, I attended monthly gatherings of top-level staff from various Jewish youth organizations.

I mentioned earlier the minor festival of *Tu B'Shevat*. In 1977 in New York, I was invited to a meeting that day, in which most of the other participants were rabbis. The theme of the meeting was the flight of many young Jews to cults, including Hare Krishna. Many of the rabbis noted that their young congregants were searching for spirituality and not finding it within Jewish synagogue life. It seemed strange to me that none of the speakers made any reference at all to *Tu B'Shevat*, which subsequently has become very popular among spiritually minded Jews, especially for its ties with nature and ecology. There wasn't even a piece of dried fruit to be seen on the table. Perhaps what was most disappointing was that so many of the rabbis complained that these young people wanted to talk about God, and the rabbis felt inadequately equipped to discuss that issue.

In 1980, after seven years of two groups each year (from the Northern and Southern Hemispheres,) I decided to leave the *Machon* and enlist in the Army education corps. I found after a while that seventeen-to-nineteen year-olds had a limited number of issues that kept recurring, year after year. For the rest of my career, I specialized in adult education. Adults have a much broader age range and a much greater – and to me, more fascinating – range of issues with which they are grappling.

There was an additional reason that began to make my work at the *Machon* more difficult. As the head of the English-speaking department, I had lots of participants who came from the Socialist Zionist youth movements. Their movement representatives in Israel insisted that after the study period in Jerusalem, they devote the second half of the year to working on a kibbutz. Some of the young people were interested in spending at least part of the time in a development town. The educational challenge of working with immigrants and bridging social and cultural gaps appealed to them. Having had similar experiences of my own in the previous decade, I could identify with their desire. Without interfering with their choices, I encouraged them to pursue these plans. I also felt that we needed to strengthen the Jewish components of the study program. Some of the movement reps attacked not only my views but me personally. I remember one who told me: "*You* are what's wrong with this Institute." In retrospect, seeing what happened in the ensuing years to the Kibbutz movement and to Labor Zionism in general, I think they should apologize to me. Israel could use a great deal more of the spirit of Young Judaea – which certainly was less dogmatic and maybe even "wishy-washy," but promoted tolerance, pluralism and democracy.

In the 1970s, I became an aunt for the first time. Judy gave birth to two sons, Nitzan and then Nadav. In the 1980s, her two daughters were born – my nieces, Michal and then Merav. The four of them – and their children – are a source of joy, challenges, worry, pride and satisfaction. I can't imagine my life in Israel without this family framework.

As a new *olah*, I confronted the polarization of the Modern Orthodox community into right and left wings. The divisive issue was the future of the territories that had been acquired/liberated/occupied (pick one, based on your political outlook) in 1967. For some of my colleagues, this represented a Messianic opportunity to fulfill their maximalist Zionist dreams of the Greater Land of Israel. In 1974, a new movement was founded called *Gush Emunim*, "Bloc of the Faithful." They were the initial kernel of the settlement movement in the West Bank – Judea and Samaria – and in Gaza. Almost immediately, those of us within the religious community who opposed them both politically and ideologically founded a much smaller group called *Oz V'Shalom* ("Strength and Peace"). We based ourselves on the verse from Psalms 29:11, "The Lord will give strength to His people; the Lord will bless His people with peace." One of the founders of that group was Mike Rosenak. The secular peace movement, *Shalom Achshav* ("Peace Now"), didn't get started until 1978.

So we spent a major chunk of our time in the 1970s debating the meaning of Zionism in general and religious Zionism in particular, and the need for Israel to live at peace with her neighbors. Many of our discussions involved Jewish attitudes to the Other. It was still early for many of us to talk of a Palestinian state – we envisioned something closer to the plan for territorial compromise suggested by the-then Foreign Minister Yigal Allon. But we were deeply concerned for the future of Israel as a Jewish and democratic state, and felt that widespread settlement of the territories would jeopardize that.

Allon died suddenly in 1980, Sadat was assassinated in 1981, the First Lebanon War broke out in 1982. Our religious peace movement was always small, never managed somehow to keep up with all the rapidly unfolding events – but, in retrospect, we were right, almost prescient.

Jewish Identity

M Y BOBBIE FELA, whom I introduced earlier, used to tell a story about her childhood in Poland. Her father, my great-grandfather, Avigdor Srebnik, was a deeply religious man who belonged to the Gerer Hasidim, and a bit of a tyrant in his home. Fela was a rebel and a Socialist-Zionist. It seems as though he practically disowned her. At the time, he was anti-Zionist, as were many Orthodox Jews in Eastern Europe. In Poland, lots of Jewish families kept fish in the bathtub when they were preparing to grind them up for gefilte fish (which leads me to believe that they didn't bathe daily!) I remember her telling a story in which her father took a fish out of the bathtub and struck her with it, because she had joined the Zionists.

But he apparently mellowed a bit and joined the Religious Zionists later in his life, after my grandparents had left Poland for the West. What she mainly told me about him is that on the eve of their departure – I picture it like the farewell scene between father and daughter in *Fiddler on the Roof* – he took her aside and whispered in her ear a Yiddish phrase, "Fela, *bleib a Yid*." (Remain a Jew.) This story had a great impact on the development of my own Jewish identity.

In the late 70s, I became the Assistant Director of the Institute for Youth Leaders, which I have mentioned above. I had primary responsibility for all the English-speaking programs at the Institute. The Director was an Argentinean, a totally secular Zionist, who had been living in Israel for many years. We often disagreed on educational issues, but we did share something very deep in common. He, too, had had a special grandmother. When he was a little boy, every night before he went to sleep, his grandmother would come into his room and tell him stories about princes, animals, fairies, and so on. But before she kissed him goodnight, every story would end with the same line, "Oscar, never forget that you're a Jew."

I learned this story from him when the American TV series "Roots" came to Israel. The Israeli staff members of the Institute told us that they had less identification with the series than we did. Because they have grown up as the majority, their Jewishness may be more natural or organic and often even taken for granted. But Oscar (Yisrael) and I felt a deep kinship with Kunta Kinte, the traditional storyteller, who preserves the family narrative and shares it with the future generations. He reminded us of our grandmothers.

Those of us who taught at the *Machon* in the 1970s always felt that we were in the shadow of the great educators who had preceded us. The teachers during the 1960s – Mike Rosenak, Haim Avni, Giddy Shimoni – all later to become professors at the Hebrew University – were legendary, and we felt very inadequate. But once, I was doing some archival research, and I saw that in the early 1940s, there had been a framework that later developed into the *Machon*. In that framework, the teacher for Zionism had been David Ben-Gurion, and for Judaism, Martin Buber!

The Talmud in *Rosh Hashanah* 25b says that "Jephtha in his generation is like Samuel in his." In other words, in each generation there's a judge – some more outstanding than others. We just have to do our best.

Although over the years, I have experienced alienation from some aspects of my Israeli identity, I have never for a moment wavered from my primal Jewish identity. I suppose you could say it was re-enforced by my surroundings. But I don't mean this in an antisemitic way. I could count on one hand the number of times I've experienced antisemitism directly, and I might have one or two fingers left over. But I do have a memory from kindergarten, when the teacher baked cookies for everyone in the class in the shape of Christmas trees. She gave me a cookie in the shape of a Star of David. On the one hand, this was a kind and thoughtful gesture on the teacher's part. On the other hand, it only served to underscore my difference from everyone else.

I should add a reservation to what I have just written. Perhaps there was one such moment, when I wavered. It was in 1999, when a friend of mine and I were traveling in Denmark. We were visiting the small, picturesque fishing village of Gilleleje, on the northern coast. I later learned that this part of Denmark is called Zealand, but this was five years before I ever visited New Zealand. Gilleleje is the place from which, in 1943, the Danish Jews were loaded onto boats and transported to safety in neutral Sweden. There is a museum that memorializes this event. After going to the Museum, my friend and I spent some time walking through the village. It was a late August day, and the sun was shining. It was warm, but not hot, with no humidity to speak of. The cloudless sky was bright blue and contrasted beautifully with the green shrubs and grass and the well-kept gardens of the residents. A few people were getting around on bicycles, so there was no engine noise. It was seductively quiet and idyllic. I began to fantasize about coming to Gilleleje for my retirement. Could I live in such a small town, without a Jewish community?

At that moment, we walked into the harbor. In the harbor of Gilleleje there is a statue, by an Israeli sculptor, of a figure blowing the Shofar, the ram's horn. The name of the statue, even in Danish, is "*T'ka B'shofar Gadol.*" It means "Sound the great Shofar" and is a phrase from a prayer which we recite daily, "Sound the great Shofar for our freedom," and which goes on to petition God for the ingathering of the exiles to the Land of Israel.

I learned recently that an Israeli tycoon had donated the sculpture about two years earlier, a replica of a statue in Herzliya, Israel. But at that moment, I had two thoughts: 1) as lovely as this Danish fishing village is, my place is with my people, in Israel. 2) The Hebrew date of this day was *Rosh Hodesh Elul*, the beginning of the month of *Elul*. On this day, traditional Jews begin to blow the Shofar in synagogue. They blow it every day leading up to Rosh Hashanah, when that is the chief commandment of the festival. What an amazing way for me to remember that.

But I can't end this reminiscence on a totally happy note. I have noted earlier that my family, and now I'm focusing on my father, were great proponents of Jewish solidarity. I remember once he said – although he was probably almost as far as possible as it is to be from *Haredim* – that any attack on a Jew *as a Jew*, including an attack on a *Haredi* Jew, he felt as a personal attack on him.

My father died in 1993, and I missed him terribly in 1994, when Baruch Goldstein perpetrated a massacre on Muslim worshippers in the Cave of the *Machpela*. I wanted so much to ask my father about the limits of Jewish solidarity. But by then he was gone, and I couldn't consult with him. So I've basically had to struggle with this question myself.

Experiences in the IDF and After

F ROM 1980 TO 1982, I served in the Israel Defense Force, with the honorary rank of captain. In those days, the Army had a program – and I don't know if it still exists – through which professionals could volunteer for service in their fields without going through the conventional challenges of basic training and officers' training. If you had a BA, you would be made an honorary lieutenant; an MA, a captain; and a Ph.D., a major. I had an MA in sociology and became an education officer. I spent two years planning and running educational programs for officers, NCO's, and officers-in-training. I had already lived in Israel for eight years, but those two years – 1980 to 1982 – did wonders for my "Israeliness," Hebrew slang, and general acclimatization.

Even with the special rank for professionals and academics, it wasn't so easy for me to enlist. The Israeli Army is divided into *sadir*, the regular conscription for 2–3 years; *keva*, the standing Army for career soldiers; and *milu'im*, the Reserves. I may have been the first person in the history of the IDF to enlist in *keva* without having done either of the other two. At first, I didn't have a serial number, and there was a whole series of bureaucratic issues to be resolved before I could finally get my uniform. For the first four months of my service, although I was working and even – hard to believe! – receiving my officer's salary, I was still serving in civilian clothes. The funny thing is that women in the Army who are pregnant can serve in their maternity clothes and not in uniform. I guess many of the people I worked with just assumed that I was pregnant.

The author as an officer in the IDF, 1980-1982

Several years later, I found that the university bureaucracy was even worse. After my first year as a doctoral student, I wasn't ready yet to submit my research proposal and needed to ask for an extension. I went to the office for Ph.D. students and they sent me to an office for people who graduated from non-Israeli schools. They didn't understand what I was doing there and sent me somewhere else. The Hebrew University in Jerusalem is spread out over several campuses in different parts of the city, and I think I must have gone to them all, with the exception of the medical school. After months of this – valuable time in which I should have been doing my research – I finally ended up in the first place I started, the office for doctoral students. The following conversation took place between the clerk and me:

D:"I can't believe that I'm the first person in the history of this university to request an extension."

C: "No, of course not; many people do. But they all work at the University."

D: "So do I."

C: "You never told me that."

D: "You never asked."

Israeli clerks almost never volunteer any information. They also don't often ask the right questions; we have to learn to do that. I got my extension and did my doctorate, but I'm jumping ahead of the story.

In the spring of 1981, my commanding officer told me that the following week, I would be attending a meeting with an officer from the West German Army. His responsibility in that army was the motivation and morale of the troops, and he was coming to Israel on his own, to learn from our experience. For a while, I agonized over the task, wondering if this German Army man might have been a former Nazi. Then, I realized he couldn't possibly have been old enough for that. Additionally, if he was coming to Israel to learn from Israeli military personnel, it was highly unlikely that he had any sympathies at all in the National Socialist direction.

It was only later, through my inter-religious dialogue work, that I began to learn about the very positive attitudes of many contemporary Germans to the Jewish people and to Israel. But during the meeting, I had a strange thought: my maternal grandparents, whom I referred to earlier as Bobbie and Zeide, left Poland in 1919. Both of them had siblings who perished in the Holocaust. If, 40 years earlier, someone had gone up to, say, my grandfather's brother, in the concentration camp, and had said, "Forty years from now, your brother's granddaughter will be sitting in Jerusalem, which will be the capital of the Jewish state. She will be wearing the uniform of the Israel Defense Force. Across from her will be sitting a German officer, and he will be asking her for advice on building a strong Army. I think that poor, unfortunate camp inmate would have said, 'Stop! This is crazy. It's what the Bible calls "mocking the poor." (Proverbs 17:5) Isn't it bad enough that I'm suffering like this – why must you also pour salt on my wounds?'"

That thought led me to ponder the challenge of the Jewish people, who went from abject powerlessness to relative power in less than a generation. If the choice is between powerlessness and power, I choose the latter. But it, too, brings with it formidable moral and ethical challenges.

There is a distinction to be drawn between using power for self-defense and inflicting punishment as an act of revenge. Or, as a friend of mine put it, "Zionism means that the Jews must get our hands dirty.

But there's a difference between getting your hands dirty and wallowing in the mud."

To be completely candid, I have to admit that one of my motivations for going into the Army at the age of 33 was I thought at the time that it would provide me with a possibility to meet some good men. Unfortunately, the good ones I met in the Army were all married. I did make one close friend and, although we don't see enough of each other, I cherish his friendship to this day. During the two years I served, I learned a great deal – don't they always say that about teachers? The programs I led dealt with Zionism, Jewish identity, Israel-Diaspora relations, Israeli politics and society, and the Arab-Israeli conflict. For three months prior to the elections – there were elections in 1981 – we weren't allowed to deal with such controversial issues. Instead, we did programs on Science and Technology, the Role of Women in Israeli Society, and other topics perceived as less politically "hot." We were not "politruks" and the programs we ran, I sincerely believe, were education and not indoctrination. We always presented a range of alternatives and encouraged critical thinking. For example, when it came to the West Bank and Gaza, we brought in a variety of speakers who each advocated a different course of action for Israel – maintenance of the status quo, annexation, the Allon plan and a Palestinian state. Long before it became fashionable to talk about two states for two peoples, we were presenting that as an option within our programs. We had a whole pool of lecturers who would come to us as their Army Reserve duty. We also tried different, more experiential methods, including simulations, games and role plays.

I feel that our programs were successful, at least in the short run. I know that I was responsible for exposing IDF officers, often for the first time in their lives, to non-Orthodox rabbis, Israeli Arabs, ultra-Orthodox Jews, Russian immigrants, even visits to kibbutzim. For me, my army service exposed me for the first time to Druze. When we ran programs in and about Jerusalem, we brought the soldiers to visit Christian and Muslim sites, as well as Jewish ones, of course. I learned recently that this practice has been discontinued – what a pity.

Sometimes there was resistance to what I was trying to communicate. I remember one group of officers-in-training to whom I was trying to explain Zionism. One of them, a Sabra, said that his Zionism consists of his having been born in Israel. I then asked how he sees me, a Zionist immigrant, or *olah*. He said, "You're a guest in my home." That seemed to me to be the opposite of classical Zionism as I understood it. The fulfillment of Zionism for a Diaspora Jew is to make *Aliyah*. That literally means "ascent" and suggests that a Jew who lives in Israel has ascended, not necessarily geographically, but spiritually and culturally. I learned from Rabbi Yoel Bin Nun that the Law of Return suggests that all Israeli Jews, including Sabras, should be thought of as people who made *Aliyah*.

In general, our method was to raise questions, complicate and even problematize. For many of our "students," it meant that for the first time, they had to think about things which they had taken for granted all their lives. During the First Lebanon War, we sent some lecturers to speak to the troops and try to make some sense of the morass of Lebanon. We did get some complaints that their complex explanations were undermining the fighting spirit of the soldiers. I know that years later, much of the educational work that we used to do in an open, liberal fashion has been taken over by the Army Rabbinate. This is part of a general intensification of the religious aspects of the IDF and concomitant with that, the highly politicized nature of the Army Rabbinate, in a right-wing direction. The work is now done in a totally different way, in a way that frightens me. In the last few rounds of fighting in Gaza, there have been commanders who appeared to have turned the war into a religious war. Even back in the early 80s, we had problems with Army rabbis. Some of them didn't want to be in programs led by a woman. We also had different kinds of problems with two other groups: flight instructors from the Air Force and physicians from the Medical Corps. In the two latter groups, many of them seemed to feel that they already knew anything worth knowing and weren't open to learning anything new. In this, they were exceptions.

But there were also programs in which I felt humbled. We had evenings that were called *Shorashim* – "Roots." People would be encouraged to bring in artifacts, pictures and stories about their families and about how they came to be in Israel. I remember one such evening, in which a Yemenite officer described how, as a young boy, he had walked with his family for two years, across the sands of Yemen, to the port at Sana'a. Another, from Iraq, told us about how his brother had been hanged in the public square in Baghdad on the charge of Zionism. What could I say? That I got on a plane and a few hours later, I landed in Israel?

The last month of my Army service coincided with the first month of the Lebanon War, 1982. Had I wanted to continue my military career, I would have had to do an abbreviated basic training and a proper officers' training course. I decided that serving for two years – which most women in the Army do – was enough, and I left the Army, for the University and, eventually, a doctoral program in Jewish education.

In retrospect, I'm grateful for the experiences I had in the Army. The exemption from service of most ultra-Orthodox men is a hot political issue in Israel. I personally was a supporter of *Hok Tal*, a law from 2002 that proposed a gradual process of integrating ultra-Orthodox men into the Army. Israel doesn't yet have a full constitution, but laws can still be declared unconstitutional by our Supreme Court, and that is what happened in 2012. The Tal Law, they maintained, violated the principle of equality.

That may be true, but drafting these men into the Army leads to violations of the principle of equality for women. The presence of more and more Orthodox men in the Army makes it harder for women's roles to be enhanced. It also has other problematic implications for the character of the Army. I do think it's very important to get more ultra-Orthodox men (and Arab women) into the labor force, but I would not insist on their serving first in the Army. That makes me somewhat unusual in the political camp I have chosen.

After two years of service, during which political activism was prohibited, I rejoined the religious peace movement I had helped found in the 1970s, *Oz V'Shalom*. Never a large group, we felt the need, in 1982, for a broader base. We joined together with other like-minded, although generally more centrist people, and founded a new group called *Netivot Shalom*. The name means "Paths of Peace" and is taken from Proverbs 3:17, referring to the Torah, "Her ways are ways of pleasantness, and all her paths are peace." In the late 1980s, the two groups more or less merged, but neither was willing to give up on its name or verse, so we combined the two.

In 1985, an historic meeting took place in the West Bank Jewish settlement of Ofra. Members of *Gush Emunim* met for the first of a series of dialogues with religious Zionists from Jerusalem, members of the religious peace movements. The dialogues were later published in book form.

At the first meeting, there were ten participants – eight men, two women. One of the men, a new immigrant, was the former Chief Rabbi of Ireland; among the other seven, all native Israelis, were two other rabbis, a member of the Knesset, educators and journalists. And the two women? Sharon (Shifra in Hebrew) Album Blass, Barnard '72, and I, Barnard '70. Shifra at the time was a resident of the Ofra settlement and a spokesperson for *Gush Emunim*.

During the meeting, I passed a note to Shifra: "I think it's significant that the only two women who are taking part in this discussion are Barnard graduates." She wrote back: "I think it's interesting that the two Barnard women saw the virtues of the other side's arguments." We agreed that the ability to listen to the other side honestly and with tolerance, while remaining passionately committed to our own side, is a quality we developed during our Barnard years.

During this period of the early 1980s, and especially through our community (see: Chapter 26), I came to know several families who had young children. In a few cases, I became a kind of ersatz aunt to these children. I used to give out ice cream to the kids who visited me on Shabbat. One year, Avinoam and Devorah knocked on my door after their first week of first grade. They wanted to tell me about school. I sat with them, listened and served ice cream. What a treat for me! Twenty years later, I became an ersatz great-aunt to a new generation of children. Many of these children, although born in Israel, have their families abroad, so that I became almost a substitute grandparent for some of them. It affords me an opportunity to see all the animated or action films I want to see – I have an excuse. I have also prepared a few kids for their Bar or Bat Mitzvah, mostly helping them put together their speeches.

I decided to continue my studies in the field of Jewish women's social and educational history. If I had wanted to continue researching Jewish education in Poland, I would probably have had to acquire at least a reading knowledge of Polish; I had no desire to do that. It made sense to "bring my topic on *Aliyah*," so to speak. I undertook to do research on five schools in Jerusalem. The focus would be on Jerusalem during the period of British rule, 1918–1948 and, specifically, on five schools attended by religious Jewish girls. One of them was the local version of *Bais Yaakov*; only now that it was in the Land of Israel, it would be known as *Bet Yaakov*, using Hebrew. While all the schools were defined as Orthodox, they nevertheless represented different ideologies and different approaches to the question of girls' education. One of them was co-educational.

I had some wonderful experiences doing the research for my dissertation, during the late 1980s and early 1990s. I will mention one: I visited a very *Haredi* girls' school in Jerusalem, called today *Bais Yankev Yoshon* (literally, "Old *Bet Yaakov*," to distinguish it from the more modern, Hebrew-speaking *Bet Yaakov*.) The original name was "*HaHeder shel Ben-Zion Yadler*," and it was founded in 1921. Yadler was the basis for a rather unpleasant character in Nobel Prize winner S. Y. Agnon's novel, *Only Yesterday*, Reb Gronem Yekum Purkan, who is generally seen through the eyes of the dog, Balak.

I made an appointment with the school's headmistress to interview her. Before I went, I had to think about how I would dress. I didn't want to put on a costume. I would dress modestly, respecting the standards of the neighborhood, but I would wear only my own clothes. I do own some long skirts and long-sleeved shirts. It was, therefore, much easier to do the research in the winter – I don't know what I would have worn in the summer. I decided to leave my Army jacket at home. When I arrived at the school, I noticed that although Yiddish was the official language of the school, the pupils were playing outside, in Hebrew. This was, of course, paradoxical, because the campaign of the anti-Zionist *Haredim* against the revival of Hebrew as a modern, spoken language stemmed from their desire to preserve its sanctity as the holy tongue.

The principal received me cordially. She asked what language I wanted to speak. I told her that I know Yiddish, but that my Hebrew is better. She spoke fluent Israeli Hebrew. Unfortunately, at the outset, I made one big mistake. I wanted to tell her that I was doing research on religious girls' education. I used the word *hokeret*, which can mean "researcher" but it can also mean "investigator." In the secular world, it has a positive connotation. In her world, as she explained to me, it generally refers to the police or the tax authorities. It took me a good twenty minutes to explain that she could trust me and that whatever I learned wouldn't be used against her or her community. In retrospect, I should have used the word *lomedet*, which means, "I am studying." Finally, she asked if I need this for *parnassa* – i.e., in order to earn a living. When I answered in the affirmative, she became very forthcoming and cooperative.

After about two hours of deep conversation, she began to inquire about setting me up with a *shidduch*, a match! Interestingly, during the times we were briefly interrupted by teachers coming in with questions, all of those exchanges were in Yiddish.

During the 1984 Knesset elections, I had an experience that brought my academic knowledge into a real-life situation. One of the interesting issues about which I have both learned and taught is the Jewish legal question of women's suffrage. I suppose in this – as in many other things – I'm really acting as my father's daughter. (He had wanted to research that topic for his doctoral dissertation.) There is a fascinating pair of Rabbinic Responsa by Rabbi Abraham Isaac HaKohen Kook (1865–1935) and Rabbi BenZion Meir Hai Uziel (1880–1953.) Both of these men served as Chief Rabbis – respectively, the first Chief *Ashkenazi* Rabbi of the Land of Israel and the first Chief *Sephardi* Rabbi of the State of Israel. Rav Kook opposed women's suffrage. Rav Uziel supported it, but indicated that by the time he wrote his responsum (1940) the issue had resolved itself.

In 1984, I organized a group of traditionally observant Jews to be poll-watchers for the Labor Party in the election held that summer. In Israel, each major party sends a representative to each polling place. The hope is that the presence of people from competing parties will prevent cheating and tampering with the votes. The Labor Party then was an overwhelmingly secular party – it became a bit less so by the 21st century (for example, in 2015, a religiously observant woman was elected to the Knesset as a Labor candidate) – and occasionally, there were problems in the polling places located in religious neighborhoods. For example, I heard that some of the secular women dressed in a manner that the religious residents considered to be immodest and caused quite a stir. So I volunteered to bring in a group of religious people – the men would be wearing skullcaps and the women would be dressed "modestly" – who identified politically with the Labor Party and could sit at the polls on Election Day. I was asked to be the chair of all the poll-watchers at one polling place in the ultra-Orthodox neighborhood of Geula.

The polling place I was asked to serve in was housed in a *Bet Yaakov* school. Almost all of the voters were *Haredim*, both men and women. The group of poll-watchers, during lulls in the voting, got to know each other by conversing about a variety of topics. I demonstrated a good knowledge of the background of the *Bet Yaakov* school system; I was dressed modestly and when we took our lunch break, I performed the ritual of hand-washing before making a blessing over the eating of my sandwich. But it was only when I mentioned that the first time I had ever voted in a municipal election, almost eleven years earlier, I had voted for a candidate from the National Religious Party – that a few people said, "What? You're religious?" In other words, the idea that a representative of the Labor Party could also be religious was so foreign to them that apparently my other acts didn't register. But having once voted for a religious party proved my credentials.

During one of these lulls, I asked the representative of the ultra-Orthodox Agudat Yisrael Party whether he was familiar with the Responsa of Rav Kook and Rav Uziel on women's suffrage. He confessed that he was not familiar with the material, and added: "It's clear that women should vote. Secular women will vote anyway. If they were to vote and our women were not, our electoral strength would be diminished by 50%!"

I do appreciate the fact that practical considerations play a role in the determination of Jewish law.

On another topic: My parents used to watch a silly comedy on TV that was called "The Love Boat." On the ship in that series, couples would meet, fall in love, break up and come together again, all within the time of a short cruise. I think that's what my parents had in mind for me in 1984, when they gave me the money to take a cruise. My mother wrote me a note, "Have a wonderful cruise – sunshine and even someone else's sonshine."

The Association of Americans and Canadians in Israel took over a Greek liner, made all the kitchens kosher, and sponsored a cruise that would be appropriate for Sabbath observers. Jewish law holds that if you're on a ship, you can stay on it over Shabbat. This particular cruise was to Venice, Dubrovnik, and several of the Greek islands, including Crete, Corfu and Santorini. I had never been to any of those places. Every day of the eight-day trip, except Shabbat, we docked at one of those venues in the morning, spent much of the day touring, sight-seeing and shopping (for me personally, not so much shopping) and came back on board in the late afternoon. On Shabbat, we had a Rabbi-in-residence, prayers, special Shabbat meals, and even a singing session, led by me.

The trip was great. It was my first and, so far, only such experience. But there was just one unattached man over the age of 18 among the

On the cruise in 1984, from left: Margalit Shilo,
the author and Varda Davidson

passengers. He was a retired professor, a widower in his 80s. I was only
37 at the time, so it wasn't exactly an appropriate match, although we
did have a drink together and I enjoyed his company. He has since
passed away.

Still, I did meet someone on that cruise who became a close friend and
colleague. Margalit at the time was a mother of five who had just finished
her doctoral dissertation, on Zionist history. Her parents gave her the
cruise as a gift. They were there, too, in their own cabin, of course.
Since her husband stayed home with the kids, she needed someone with
whom to share her cabin. I was happy to oblige.

We became good friends. I was very impressed with Margalit's knowledge of history and European culture, and even Greek mythology.
We shared common intellectual and academic interests, as well as her
budding religious feminism. I'm not sure if she would have developed as
she did without knowing me – probably, yes. But I certainly encouraged
her and she became the number one historian of women's history in
Israel. She has published several of the most important books in the

field, including one on the struggle for women's suffrage in Israel.

I'm sorry I didn't publish my dissertation. I did publish a few articles from it, but it is far less well-known than my master's thesis. Part of the problem was that I was turned down by three or four publishers. Of course, that happens, but I felt that some of the reasons given for the rejection were incomprehensible. One of them praised the originality and creativity of my work, but found it "too specific," because I focused only on Jerusalem. Had I written about girls' education throughout all of Mandatory Palestine, they said they would have considered publishing it. It seemed to me at that point that they had published far more specific books, including, for example, biographies of single individuals. It's possible that their response reflects not only on their estimation of the quality of my work, but also on what they thought in those days about the importance of women's history.

Teaching Christians and Others

I T WAS ABRAHAM JOSHUA HESCHEL who wrote, "Judaism today is the least known religion." For many years, I have had
the privilege of teaching groups of Christians who come to
Jerusalem from throughout the world. Many of them are priests,
pastors and nuns on Sabbatical; some are lay people. They come
from anywhere, stay between a week to a year, and my involvement
varies, depending on the length and depth of the program.

I teach them about Judaism and about Israel. I give introductions
to the Christians who visit our synagogue on Friday nights for prayers
and we sometimes also provide them with home hospitality for Shabbat
dinners. It is fascinating to note what questions they ask. In one case, a
young woman was surprised that our sanctuary was not decorated with
pictures of Moses. Once, I told a group of seminarians that they were
imposing Christian questions on Judaism; what interested them almost
exclusively were concepts of Messiah, the afterlife, the resurrection
of the dead and so on, things that most Jews rarely discuss. We Jews
actually devote an inordinate amount of time to discussions about food.

The questions I encounter do not seem to vary much between Prot-
estants and Catholics; but they do vary a great deal between Western
Christians, who generally know some Jews, as friends, neighbors or
colleagues, and those Asian or African Christians for whom I may be the
first Jew they have ever met. I have been asked "Are Jews still offering
animal sacrifices?" I doubt that any North American or British Christian
would ask that; Africans sometimes do. When the only Jews you know
are the ones in the Old Testament, it is a legitimate question. For a

teacher, it's a wonderful opportunity to teach about how Jewish practice and Jewish life changed after the destruction of the Temple.

With a different group, I taught about what is Midrash, what is Mishna, what is *Halakha*, and something about the Jewish calendar and festivals. One of my students, an Australian Catholic, asked about what he called a "strange tension" within Judaism. Almost immediately, he changed his definition to "a dance" between two poles. One pole, according to his words: You Jews always want "to get it right"; to serve God in the most "correct" way possible. It's important to you, for example, what the correct dimensions of the Sukkah should be, when it is kosher and when it is unacceptable, and so on. But, he continued, you also play with Judaism, you laugh, you enjoy.

I think what he was referring to primarily was that (this is something I had taught them) sometimes the Midrash tells us: "Don't read the text this way, read it that way." For example, when Isaiah (54:13) says, "All your children shall be learned of the Lord, and great shall be the peace of your children," the Midrash comments: "don't read *banayikh*, 'your children,' but rather, *bonayikh*, 'your builders.'" (*Masekhet B'rakhot* 64a.) I don't know if this Australian was fully aware of what we do on Purim or on Simhat Torah. To the best of my knowledge, there is no other religious culture in the world in which this kind of innocent tomfoolery, without orgies – Purim-Torah or a Purim-Spiel – is part of the religion itself. We serve God by poking innocent fun at His Torah. We dance with it, we have fun with it. Purim-Torah mocks our sacred prayers and Scriptures; the classical Purim-Spiel may mock Biblical stories. The one in our community usually just makes fun of ourselves.

There is a story that appears in *Masekhet Ta'anit* 22a, in which Rabbi Beroka asks Elijah the Prophet which of the people going around in the market-place is destined for the World-to- Come. Elijah points to two people who say, "We are happy people and we make those who are sad, happy." The Aramaic word for "making others happy" is *m'vadhin*, parallel to *badhanim*, the jesters or jokesters known to us from Jewish folklore. To laugh and make jokes can be a religious act.

In the fall of 2010, a wonderful man who was a dear friend and colleague of mine in inter-religious dialogue, passed away. His name was Professor Brother Jack Driscoll, of blessed memory. Jack was a devout Christian who loved Judaism. He especially appreciated the character of our Sabbath and the Midrashic method of reading texts. Once we

Leadership of the ICCJ signing Berlin Document, 2009. Author is first from left in the front row. In the wheel chair is Wolfgang Schäuble, German Minister of the Interior. Photo courtesy of ICCJ.

were talking and I said that sometimes Jews have such an obsession with Halakhic detail that we lose the forest for the trees. He replied, "But at least you have trees." I never would have said that, but since a devout Catholic said it, I allow myself to repeat it. To me, that is again a kind of dance or tension between two poles.

What I love about Midrash is that it opens up possibilities of interpretation. The classic Midrash gives one interpretation; then it says, "*davar aher* – another thing; then again, *davar aher*," and so on. The same text is open to many interpretations, even when they might contradict each other.

In addition to the classes I teach, in some cases, I also take the Christian groups to visit Yad Vashem. Although I am by no means a scholar of the Shoah, I believe I have developed an understanding of how Christians experience Yad Vashem. On only one occasion was I told "I have Holocaust fatigue." Most of the Christians feel a deep sense of responsibility and sometimes even guilt. They immediately apply these feelings to contemporary situations in their own countries.

One of the problems with Yad Vashem is that the historical museum stresses the long history of Christian antisemitism as the background for the rise of modern antisemitism and the Holocaust. But then at no point does it mention any of the significant changes that have occurred within the Church during the last fifty years.

Another related topic about which I teach is the Jewish-Christian relationship itself, the dialogue. An important document in the history of the relationship is the Ten Points of Seelisberg (see Appendix A) written by a group of Jews and Christians in 1947 – the year of my birth – who laid the foundations for what became the International Council of Christians and Jews, of which I served as President from 2008 to 2014. During my term of office, we produced another document called "A Time for Recommitment," usually called "The Berlin Document." We wanted to update the points of Seelisberg, not only because of significant changes that had occurred in the ensuing six decades, but also because in 1947, all of the points were directed at Christians. Did the Jews have no responsibility at all for improving and enhancing the relationship?

The entire document is, I think, definitely worth reading – I'm not exactly objective – but the best-known section is the Twelve Calls of Berlin (See Appendix B) which include four calls to Christians and the churches, four calls to Jews and Jewish communities, and four calls for joint action. I have taught this document on six continents. It is quite controversial, especially in Jewish settings. I believe it may be the first time that Christians and Jews have been self-critical in each other's presence. We have been accused by some Jews of washing our dirty laundry in public. To this, I have a double response: (1) In the digital age, it's no longer so clear what the boundaries are between the public and the private spheres; (2) If I have a choice between washing my dirty laundry in public or going around with stinky laundry, I'd rather wash it in public. Many Jews have disagreed with that.

As Christians are learning more about Judaism, I think that Jews have to become much more knowledgeable about Christianity, including some familiarity with the New Testament. I have often thought it strange that Jews, who are very quick to claim athletes, politicians and movie stars, not to mention Nobel laureates, as Jews – we sometimes play a kind of game, "Did you know that so-and-so is Jewish?" – generally ignore the most famous and arguably the most important Jew who ever lived, Jesus of Nazareth. Jews and Christians will never see Jesus in the same way; that is one of the most important differences between us.

Yet I do think that more Jews should recognize Jesus as a great Jewish teacher and spiritual personality.

I mentioned before that my experience in dialogue goes beyond the Christian-Jewish relationship. One of the amazing discoveries for me has been what Jews share in common with Hindus – for example, a similar attachment to our respective homelands. One of my dialogue partners insists that Hinduism at its heart is monotheistic, and that the many deities are manifestations of the central Godhead, an idea that echoes some strands of Jewish mysticism, or Kabbalah. Any similarities between the Hindu and Jewish traditions are not likely to be the product of historical interaction, so that makes them even more interesting to me.

I had my first – and, so far, only – experience in India in 2006. Although I was there for only ten days, I felt that it was the equivalent of a much longer journey – not at all because it was tedious, which it wasn't. It was so packed full of sensory bombardment, surprises, people, stories, fears, joy and contrasts, that I felt I had been there for much longer.

For seven years, beginning in 2002, I was privileged to be part of an international, inter-religious think tank called "Thinking Together," under the auspices of the World Council of Churches. We generally met once or twice a year. In 2006, we were invited to hold our second meeting of that year in an ashram, led by my Hindu physician friend whom I mentioned at the beginning of the memoir. The meeting in the ashram was scheduled for *Hol HaMoed Sukkot*, one of the intermediary days of the Feast of Booths. At first, I hesitated to travel during that time. I would have to travel with the "Four Species" – palm frond, citron, myrtle and willow – that we use for the special ritual of prayers on the intermediary days, and who knows if I could get them through customs? The festival ends with a major celebration, *Sh'mini Atzeret – Simhat Torah*, and I hadn't been away from my community in Jerusalem for that festival in more than two decades. In Israel, the two festivals are conflated into one day; in the Diaspora they are two separate days, back-to-back. Several of the members of our dialogue group tried to persuade me to go because they said that our meeting was scheduled to end on Friday – I could travel to Cochin in a few hours and make it in time to spend the festival with the small Jewish community there. Realizing that this might be a once-in-a-lifetime opportunity, I decided to make the trip.

There were some magical moments in the ashram, including a party to celebrate the end of our meeting, with Indian music and dancing. The strongest beverage served was pistachio milk. I remarked to one of my Christian friends there that if we're having so much fun on just pistachio milk, can you imagine what it would be like if they served alcohol?

The next morning, several young Hindus from the ashram drove me to Cochin. I had booked a room in the one hotel that is within walking distance of the one functioning synagogue in that dwindling community. Friday night, which was also the night of *Sh'mini Atzeret*, I decided to pray and eat by myself, in the hotel room, since I didn't feel safe walking alone at night. The streets are not well-lit and there are all kinds of animals in the street – not only "sacred cows," but chickens, goats, etc. Even without the animals, traffic is crazy – hundreds of motor scooters with several people piled on top of each, zigzagging through the rest of the vehicular traffic.

The next morning, I walked to the synagogue. It took me about twenty minutes. The neighborhood is called Jewtown and the street is called Synagogue Lane. Interestingly, both what look like swastikas and what look like Stars of David are symbols in Indian art and the synagogue had buildings near it with each of those symbols. The visit to the synagogue was for me less a religious experience and more of an anthropological one. They did have a Kiddush, a collation, after the service, with tasty Indian food. I was thinking of going back that evening for the *Simhat Torah* celebration. As an Israeli, I would no longer be bound by the Jewish legal prohibitions of the festival and could perhaps take a taxi from the hotel. But, at nightfall, it started to rain very hard – it was the beginning of the monsoon season – and I just didn't feel like going out. I resolved to attend the next morning, so as not to miss the Diaspora celebration altogether, but to stay inside that evening and watch some television.

There were a number of channels that showed Western films. To my surprise and joy, the film that had been chosen for that evening on one of the channels was Barbra Streisand in "Yentl," the story by Isaac Bashevis Singer about a young woman in Eastern Europe who cross-dresses as a man in order to be able to study Talmud in a Yeshiva! Jews being slightly more than 0% of the total population of India, I must assume that this was only a funny coincidence.

The first time I saw "Yentl," when it came out in 1983, I thought to myself, "Someone has made a film based on my dissertation, even before I've written it."

The next day, when I took part in the *Hakafot*, the processions with Torah scrolls, I saw that women are involved more than in many Orthodox settings; not carrying the scrolls, but at least following the procession. In the afternoon *Minha* service, the Torah procession goes outside and the congregants march around the synagogue.

I used to say that India is everything and its opposite: It's beautiful and ugly; serene and calm, as well as noisy and chaotic; both fragrant and malodorous. I felt as though my senses were being barraged, all at once. I experienced there some of the most beautiful views, lush vegetation, helpful and pleasant people, delicious vegetarian food, that I've ever encountered in my life. At the same time, some of the most squalid living conditions I've ever seen and some of the filthiest toilets, even in institutions of higher learning. It's hard to make sense of all of that.

When I came back from India, I organized for our synagogue an evening of Indian food, music, pictures, and – mainly – stories. My plan was that I would speak for 20–30 minutes and then open the floor, not only for questions, but also for participation by members of the community who had had more significant experiences there, some for several months, one for up to a year. I started speaking and when I looked down at my watch, I saw that an hour and twenty minutes had passed! So, I quickly brought the evening to a close. But I suppose that I could have gone on . . .

It Might Lead to Mixed Dancing

PART ONE: HAVDALAH

As I have mentioned, I love folk dancing, especially Israeli folk dancing. I learned this mostly in the Young Judaea camp both as a camper and then later a counselor. One of the things we did in camp – actually, many Jewish summer camps do this – is to hold the *Havdalah* ceremony outside, weather permitting, and then to finish with dancing in wide circles.

First, a short explanation about the ceremony itself: *Havdalah* – literally, separating, dividing or making distinctions – is not only a basic element of Jewish culture; it is the way in which the Torah says that the world was created. Already in Genesis 1:3, ". . . and God divided the light from the darkness." Subsequently, God divides the lower waters from the upper waters (v. 7) and the day from the night (v. 14). In our Jewish lives, we distinguish between the sacred and the profane, the pure and the impure, the permitted and the forbidden. The Hebrew word for wisdom, *binah*, comes from the word *bein*, "between," since wisdom consists largely of being able to draw distinctions between different things.

Havdalah is also the name of the beautiful ceremony we perform at the end of the Shabbat, to make a distinction between the end of this wonderfully special day and the resumption of our working week. As we inaugurated the Shabbat with candles and wine, so, too, do we end it with candles and wine, but also with spices, so that the beauty and sweetness of the day we have just experienced might continue to make our lives pleasant, even during the mundane week ahead. The *Havdalah* candle is a special, braided one, symbolically uniting the two candles we lit to usher in the Shabbat on Friday. Thus, the four distinctions mentioned in the main blessing of *Havdalah* (i.e., between the holy and the profane, between light and darkness, between Israel and the nations, between the seventh day and the six days of work) are not necessarily impermeable ones.

Some of us have trouble with a notion of rigid separation between Jews and non-Jews. As is written in the Hirsch Siddur and quoted in the Jewish Catalog I, "That which is set apart from other things as 'holy' is so distinguished only in order that it may imbue with holiness and consecration also every phase of life taking place beyond its confines . . . the Seventh Day was set apart from the six working days only so that its Sabbath spirit might permeate all of weekday life." Similarly, we might hope that the distinctiveness of the Jewish people is in order to bring blessing to all the families of the earth (see Genesis 12: 3).

Many people, when they bless the *Havdalah* candle, use its light to gaze at their fingernails. There are a number of explanations for this custom, the main one being that since we don't cut our nails on Shabbat, this gives us an opportunity to see how they've grown and wonder at the miracle of growth and regeneration. Hopefully, the Shabbat will have been for us an opportunity, as well, for spiritual growth, or what Heschel called "a weekly exercise in profound living." At the end of the ceremony, we wish each other *shavua tov* – a good week – and continue, refreshed and re-created, with the rest of our lives.

In camp, we used to end the ceremony with a big *hora*. The leader of the circle would shout out some words and the group would respond. He or she would usually begin with: *Abba* – Dad, and the group would shout, *Ima* – Mom.

It would go like this:

Leader: *Abba*.

Group: *Ima*.

L: *Ima*.

G: *Abba*.

L: *Abba, Ima, Ima, Abba*.

G: *Ima, Abba, Abba, Ima*.

And so on. Sometimes we would use *Sabba* – Grandpa, and *Savta* – Grandma. And we also used opposite words like *Ken* – yes, and *Lo* – no.

That was in the 1960s and 70s. If we flash-forward to 1990, I was in Israel, and my adorable nieces, then aged 7 and 4, came to Jerusalem to spend Shabbat with me. My four nephews and nieces are all *Sabras*, born and raised in Israel. After we made *Havdalah*, I started dancing with the two little girls. I did the thing about *Abba* and *Ima*, *Sabba* and *Savta*. Then, I shouted *Ken* and they shouted back, "Barbie."

After laughing for quite a while, I realized that what they said made a lot more sense. The other two sets had been the male and female members of a couple, not opposites. So Ken and Barbie actually fit in well . . .

I have had two especially memorable *Havdalah* experiences. One was just outside of Stuttgart, Germany, in 2009. That was my second trip to Germany that summer. Starting in 2007, I have visited Germany more than any other country, mainly on ICCJ business. But this was a conference of European feminist theologians from the three Abrahamic faiths. The theme chosen for the conference was a quotation from the late Caribbean-American poet and feminist theorist, Audre Lorde. Lorde wrote an essay called, "The Master's Tools Will Never Dismantle the Master's House." I was invited to be the Jewish speaker and I called my talk, "Dismantling or Renovating? The Perspective of an Orthodox Jewish Feminist." When they first invited me to participate, I explained that I had three issues that might complicate things.

The conference was scheduled to take place from Thursday to Sunday. That Wednesday evening and Thursday was the Jewish fast day, *Tisha B'Av*, the 9th of Av, commemorating the destruction of the First and Second Temples and other tragic events in Jewish history. The first issue I raised was kosher food, which they said they would provide for me. The second one was Shabbat. Participation in the conference would not involve me in any activity that would violate the laws of Shabbat, and they said that I could give my talk on Friday morning. As far as the 9th of Av was concerned, they would bring me in the day before, I could attend synagogue for the service and reading of Lamentations and, as it is permitted to travel on all fast days with the exception of Yom Kippur, I could then arrive at the conference a few hours before breaking the fast. All of this seemed very accommodating, and I agreed to the offer. The conference would be held at a retreat center just outside of Stuttgart, but too far to attend Shabbat services at the synagogue. On Shabbat, I would have to pray by myself.

Spending the eve of *Tisha B'Av* in the cavernous but almost-empty synagogue in Stuttgart seemed eerily appropriate – a once-sizable Jewish community that had been destroyed. There were a handful of elderly male worshippers downstairs on the main floor and three slightly younger women (around my age) upstairs. I remembered that the Classical Jewish Reformers in the early 19th century had said, "Stuttgart is my Jerusalem." An acquaintance of mine from Jerusalem was one of the women in the synagogue. It turned out that she goes to Germany almost every summer for another inter-religious study program, and she had prepared the delicious kosher food I would be eating at the conference.

Of the twenty-five or so participants in the conference, there was to be one other Jewish woman, an Israeli named Rivka who had been living in Germany for about thirty years, and she would share the Shabbat observance with me. She and I had been asked to lead a Shabbat experience for the women theologians Friday evening, with songs, explanations and Torah study. We began by teaching the group a widely-known song that it's customary to sing at the beginning of the Shabbat table ritual – "*Shalom Aleikhem*." This is a cognate of the phrase "*Salaam Aleikum*" in Arabic and means, "peace be unto you." The words have been set to many different tunes – I personally know at least four or five – but we chose to teach the best-known, a simple, catchy tune.

Shabbat ended up being quite a pleasurable experience. I met some fascinating women, including several who had been ordained as Catholic priests and then were promptly excommunicated by the Vatican. Two of them were even appointed as bishops. It turns out that outside the official Roman Catholic establishment, there is a world-wide network of more than 100 (maybe by now it's even more) women serving as priests. I must add that the weather was beautiful and we spent a good deal of time outdoors. The kosher food was tasty, I enjoyed getting to know Rivka – we spoke in Hebrew part of the time – and in general Shabbat was restful and fun, as it should be.

In the summer, with daylight savings time, Shabbat ends quite late. This particular Shabbat was scheduled to end around 10 p.m. The conference program included an international folk dance session that was supposed to begin around 9. I realized that I could attend: since the dance teacher would not be a Jew, she could turn on the music and I could dance to it. We went outside, on the grass, during the last hour of the day. I love dawn and dusk, much as I love the transitional seasons of spring and fall. I'm rarely up at dawn, but I do appreciate sunsets. This was a particularly beautiful sunset, leading to a clear night that was warm, but the air was dry and pleasant.

The dance session was excellent. We did a variety of dances from different cultures. The last one was going to be a special dance that we would do with candles in our hands. We were taught the dance without the music and without knowing what the origin of the dance was – it's quite possible that the teacher herself didn't know. After she taught us the steps, she began to hand out the candles. I thought it was still Shabbat, during which I couldn't hold candles. As I started to explain this to the teacher, Rivka said, "Debbie, look up at the sky!" When I did, I saw that there were three stars, a sign that Shabbat is over. I quickly said the sentence that ends the Shabbat and took one of the candles. The teacher put on the music . . . It was the tune we had taught the night before to *"Shalom Aleikhem."*

After this, Rivka and I made *Havdalah* for the whole group. It is customary at the end of *Havdalah* to sing "Have a good week . . ." in Hebrew and sometimes in Yiddish. We invited the women to add all the different languages they knew. We sang in English, French, German, Dutch, Swedish, Arabic, and some more I've forgotten.

My other *Havdalah* story is perhaps less about *Havdalah* itself but more about the story and a disturbing reaction to it. I know that many Jews find this strange, but in addition to Germany, another country I enjoy visiting and have been to four times, is Poland. Germany as a nation has gone through a long process of soul-searching and has provided us with a wonderful example of *metanoia*, transformation, or what Jews call *"teshuvah."* In Poland, this phenomenon exists but to a far lesser extent – there are individuals and groups who have gone through a similar process. Some Poles are philosemites and each summer, a major festival of Jewish culture is held in Cracow.

In the summer of 2011, the ICCJ held its annual international conference in Cracow, one of my favorite European cities. I have a personal connection to the Jewish history of that city, in that Sarah Schenirer, the founder of the *Bet Yaakov* movement, about whom I had done research in graduate school, was from Cracow. But more than that, it's a city that was not bombed during the War, and the colorful Old City has remained intact. We deliberately scheduled our conference dates to dovetail with the last few days of the culture festival. The conference typically begins on Sunday evening, and I arrived in Cracow on Thursday.

June-July in Poland can be very wet and during the conference, I went on a walking tour in the footsteps of Pope John Paul II, in the driving rain. But on Shabbat, we had fairly decent weather. I took a room in a small hotel overlooking the main square of the Old City. Saturday night would be the concluding concert of the festival, with mostly Klezmer music. Klezmer music has become very popular in Europe – among Gentiles – and I've been to Klezmer concerts in Poland, Switzerland and Hungary. The latter seemed to me more like Dixieland jazz, without the soul of Klezmer, but that doesn't seem to matter all that much, in terms of the cultural phenomenon I'm describing. Often, neither the bands nor the audiences are Jewish.

I was sitting in my hotel room at the end of Shabbat, waiting to make *Havdalah* so that I could go out into the street and join the ten thousand or so who had gathered to enjoy the concert. Most of the people who attend the festival are not Jewish. I made *Havdalah*, and then when I went out into the street, they invited a Jewish man up onto the stage – to make *Havdalah*!

I told this story to an acquaintance in Israel. She considers herself and is considered by many others, as well, to be liberal and open-minded and her response was, "That's disgusting!"

I said, "I think it's beautiful; why do you think it's disgusting?" She said, "First they kill us; then they love us?"

At first, I tried to explain that most of the concert-goers in the city square that night were young people, who were born long after the War. Secondly, I began my little speech about "*teshuvah*," but realized that it would probably not be understood. I'm truly sorry that some Jews feel that way. Perhaps if they met more real-live Poles and Germans, especially the Christians who come to the institutions at which I teach in Jerusalem, they might begin to feel differently.

Part Two: South Africa

There's a well-known Jewish joke:

Q: Why don't Orthodox Jewish couples make love standing up?
A: Because it might lead to mixed dancing.

In 1978, I was in South Africa for my first visit there. I returned under different auspices in 2011, and saw that the country had changed radically. It is a physically beautiful place, with a fascinating blend of tribal cultures. In the post-Mandela era, South Africa has multiple problems – what country doesn't? – but I felt that it was moving in a more positive direction. However, my first visit was during the height of apartheid, only two years after the riots in Soweto. The reason for my trip, as I mentioned in an earlier chapter, was to help run some educational seminars for Jewish youth. I debated with myself before I went, as I thought and still think that apartheid was one of the great evils of the 20th century. I didn't want to do anything that would support the regime. But it seemed to me that teaching Jewish youngsters about their heritage, especially if we emphasized the universal values of that heritage, could be defensible. At the least, I did make a commitment to myself that I wouldn't use a segregated toilet.

When I arrived in South Africa, I realized that all the public toilets were segregated. There was no way I could spend a month in that country and not violate my commitment. I remember going to a toilet that was "for Europeans only." I thought to myself, "I'm a former American who lives in Asia and is visiting in Africa, but I'm defined as a European."

During the month I was in South Africa, I got into trouble twice for different kinds of mixed dancing.

The first time was in the north, outside of Johannesburg. There was a comfortable, developed campsite where we held our first seminar. The staff serving in the dining room were all black Africans.

As part of the program of the seminar, we used to sing and dance after each meal, except breakfast. One day, after lunch, the dancing was especially spirited. I noticed one of the African women clapping and stamping her feet in tempo with the music. It looked to me as though she wanted to join the dance. I went over to her, took her hand, and brought her into the circle. After the dance, one of the local Jewish organizers of the program pulled me aside. He told me that what I had done was a criminal offense in that country – mixed dancing with people of different races. I apologized, explaining that I hadn't known.

If I lived in South Africa, I would have continued doing this – and probably other, even more significant "offenses" – but then I would be around to bear the consequences. I realized that at the end of the month, I would be returning to Israel, so it wasn't really fair for me to jeopardize the locals. I decided to leave my personal protest aside and continue with the educational work for which they had brought us.

Later that month, we ran a second seminar, in the south, on the Cape. It was held at a kosher hotel in a town outside of Capetown, called Muizenburg, the heart of the wine industry. In those days, the town was nicknamed "Jewsenburg." This time, I offered a workshop for the kids in Israeli folk dancing.

South African Jewry used to be called "National-Traditional." This meant that while the majority of the community were not strictly observant, they *were* traditional, and had a very strong connection with Israel. The Chief Rabbinate there is Orthodox, and the schools sponsoring our seminars were nominally Orthodox. I took pains not to teach any couple dances, but to focus exclusively on the more "innocent" circle and line dances. Somehow I forgot that in the beginners' dance *Ush'avtem mayim*, (literally, "And you shall draw forth water . . ." from Isaiah 12:3) there is one part where the people in the circle, walking into the center, generally take one another's hands.

We were doing this dance, and at that very moment, one of the Orthodox rabbis walked by. He saw a teen-aged boy take the hand of the girl who was dancing next to him. After the session, he told me that from now on, I could lead dancing only for the girls. Thus I got into trouble in South Africa twice for mixed dancing: once by race, the second time, by gender.

Shabbat and Inter-Religious Dialogue

T HE ICCJ is the International Council of Christians and Jews, based in the Martin Buber House in Heppenheim, Germany, near Frankfurt. Although I had been involved with the World Council of Churches since 1988, I didn't really know the ICCJ until 2006. It is an umbrella organization for member organizations in about thirty-four countries around the world. In 2006, I attended the international conference in Vienna and was invited back to present a keynote address the following year in Sydney. I chaired the conference that was held in Jerusalem in 2008 and it was there I was elected President of the organization. My first conference in this role was in 2009, in Berlin, where we issued the Berlin Document, "A Time for Recommitment." My second conference as President was in 2010. Since the theme of that conference was to be "trilateral dialogue," with Jews, Christians and Muslims, we decided to hold the conference in a majority Muslim country. The two possibilities we considered were Morocco and Turkey, and we settled on Turkey, which has a larger Jewish community and a significant Orthodox Christian presence.

A true moment of crisis for the ICCJ occurred on May 31, the date of the Turkish-Israeli flotilla incident at sea. This was exactly three weeks before the conference was scheduled to take place. There were some voices in our organization calling for a postponement or cancellation of the conference, which, in practical terms, would have been the same. Some of them had security fears; others felt we should boycott Turkey.

Despite the travel advisory warnings of the Israeli government, we

decided to hold the conference as planned. In our letter to the regis-
trants, we wrote: "The words of Hillel in the Ethics of the Fathers are
most appropriate: 'If not now, when?' Interfaith and peace organizations
are tested in times of crisis. Now more than ever our presence in Istanbul
is needed, and hopefully we will be able to contribute something (even
very small) to defuse tensions."

Out of the more than a hundred Jews, Christians, and Muslims,
from five continents, who had registered, six were due to come from
Israel. Three unfortunately canceled; three others came in, all on Israeli
passports. This was my fourth time in Turkey, and I felt absolutely no
difference from the other three times – neither at Ben-Gurion nor
at Ataturk Airport, nor in Istanbul itself. Our decision was proven in
retrospect to have been a correct one; the conference proceeded without
a hitch, and ended up being one of our most successful.

The opening session featured authentic Turkish music, a beautiful
DVD about Istanbul being a European Capital of Culture for 2010,
and a wonderful address by the Ecumenical Patriarch Bartholomew.
We also received greetings from the office of the Mufti and the local
Jewish community. Each day basically had the same general format: We
began with a meditative moment for the whole conference, on each day
from a different one of the three religious traditions. We then held a
plenum, featuring a keynote speaker from one of the traditions, with a
respondent from each of the other two. The theme of the keynote was
how each tradition relates to the Other. The rest of the morning on
the first two days was devoted to workshops on such topics as Muslims
in Europe, the Palestine Kairos Document, women's issues, text study,
trilateral dialogue, and comparative mysticism. On the third day, the
morning was concluded with two concurrent panels on controversial
topics, one on Turkey and the EU, the other on religion and state.
The afternoons involved outings, to tourist sites, a cathedral, a Jewish
museum and a synagogue.

One evening featured the screening of a film on Turkey's role in
saving Jewish lives during the Holocaust. After a closing session, we set
out for a beautiful boat ride on the Bosporus, capped with dinner on
the boat and a presentation of Turkish folklore. The most important
immediate result of the conference was that at our Annual General
Meeting held the morning after the conference, we decided to revive a
veteran ICCJ framework known as the Abrahamic Forum. This would

be a way of engaging Muslims, without changing the nature of the existing Councils of Christians and Jews.

The first Muslim on the Steering Committee of the Forum was my late friend and colleague, Abdesalaam Najjar, who died suddenly in March 2012, at the age of 59.[1] He was one of the founding members of *Wahat el-Salam / Neveh Shalom* (Oasis of Peace), a village not far from Jerusalem, established jointly by Jewish and Palestinian Arab citizens of Israel. The Jewish tradition says that the only prophecy left in our world is the names parents give to their children. A devout Muslim, Najjar was, as his first name suggests, a true servant of the Lord and a man of peace. Abdesalaam was the first Palestinian Israeli to move to the village, but others have joined since.

In November, 2011, the Inter-Religious Coordinating Council in Israel organized a meeting in Jerusalem with the U.S. Ambassador to Israel, Daniel B. Shapiro. Attending the meeting were interfaith activists from the Greater Jerusalem area, representing the three monotheistic traditions. After describing some of the difficulties we face in our work, we were asked by the Ambassador, "How do you maintain hope within this situation of conflict?" Abdesalaam replied, "We are living the future that we are trying to create." This was certainly true for him in the village.

Another example of this, I would say, is the Jew who hopes for redemption, while on a weekly basis, experiences the Shabbat as a foretaste of the world-to-come. The Protestant theologian Harvey Cox once wrote:

"Christian hope suggests that man is destined for a City. It is not just any city, however. If we take the Gospel images as well as the symbols of the book of Revelation into consideration, it is not only a City where injustice is abolished and there is no more crying. It is a city in which a delightful wedding feast is in progress, where the laughter rings out, the dance has just begun, and the best wine is still to be served."[2]

---

1. (Portions of) text previously published in *Co-Existence and Reconciliation in Israel: Voices for Interreligious Dialogue* (Kronish), Copyright © 2015 by the Stimulus Foundation, Inc., Paulist Press, Inc., Mahwah, NJ. Reprinted by permission of Paulist Press, Inc., www.paulistpress.com.
2. Cox, *The Feast of Fools: A Theological Essay on Festivity and Fantasy*, Harper Colophon Books: New York, 1969, p.162.

The appealing description in Cox's statement above actually happens every Friday night in a traditional Jewish home: feasting, singing, laughter, the best wine, and so on. Without the weekly taste of Shabbat, it might have been difficult for Jews to sustain a Messianic hope throughout two millennia of Diaspora life. Shabbat has become the organizing principle and anchor of my own life.

And, often because of my inter-religious work, I have spent Shabbat in all sorts of strange places, from Kotor in Montenegro, to Hiroshima in Japan, from Hofgeismar in Germany, to Bhusan in South Korea. Once, during my first trip to New Zealand, the travel agent arranged for me to spend most of a Friday traveling the length of the North Island to Wellington. He assured me we would arrive at our destination well before the onset of Shabbat. But because this was a holiday weekend, with boarding school children and soldiers trying to get home, the bus turned out to have a different route, winding in and out of every little town or village along the way. I began to get nervous. What if I didn't make it to Wellington in time for Shabbat? Could I get off the bus somewhere along the way and splurge on a taxi? The driver told me that I had no such alternative, practically.

I was sitting and looking at my watch every few minutes, and the lady sitting next to me finally asked, "I notice you keep looking at your watch. You look nervous. Is something wrong?"

I said, "Well, I'm a Sabbath observer and I'm supposed to speak this evening in the synagogue in Wellington. I'm afraid we're taking a slower route than the travel agent in Australia said, and I might be late."

"Oh, she said, "Where are you from?"

I replied, "From Israel – Jerusalem."

A few minutes later, she asked, "What religion are you?"

I tried very hard not to laugh. I had thought that my religion was obvious. But, obviously, it wasn't. And, when I was travelling in South India, I met a highly educated young man, who had a master's degree in medical sociology, but had never heard of Jews or Judaism, and seemed disturbed that I wasn't Christian or Muslim, the two categories he knew for religions outside India.

We finally arrived in Wellington. I had about twenty minutes to spare before candle-lighting. Fortunately, that morning, before setting out on the journey, I had washed my hair and had packed my Shabbat clothes on top. I rushed to the hotel which wasn't far from the bus station. The folks at Reception were surprised that I didn't want a room with a view, but rather a room on the lowest floor they could find, since I don't use the elevator on Shabbat.

Before leaving the hotel, I asked them for directions to the synagogue, which I knew wasn't far from the hotel. They asked me if I wanted to take a map with me, but I had to turn down that offer, since I don't carry on Shabbat. I wandered around in the street, asked several more people, and became worried that it was getting late. Finally, I saw a building that had a large window and it looked like there were people inside praying. I figured that they might know where the synagogue was, so I decided to go in and ask. As I walked in, they began to recite Psalm 92, "A song for the Sabbath Day." Not only was that the right place, but I made it just "in the nick of time." There is a lovely preparatory service that precedes this psalm, called *Kabbalat* Shabbat, which I missed, but the official opening of the Shabbat liturgy is Psalm 92. From then on, I enjoyed every minute of my stay in Wellington and have gone back twice since. The second time I traveled to Wellington, I made sure to visit it in the middle of the week and stay in a room on a high-enough floor to be able to see the beautiful harbor view.

One Shabbat in 2006, I stayed in a hotel in Kotor, Montenegro. It was August and very hot. The hotel had no air-conditioning. Shabbat afternoon, I became very thirsty and went to the desk in the lobby to request a bottle of water or seltzer to quench my thirst. I explained that because it's the Sabbath – of course, the receptionist had never heard of that – I can't pay for the bottle of water until nightfall. She didn't really understand and said that at least I should sign for it. I tried to explain that this, too, I was unable to do. I realized that saying "it's against my religion," which would have worked well in, say, North America, simply fell flat in this post-Communist setting. It took a few more minutes, the receptionist must have been convinced that she was dealing with a guest who was stark raving mad, but I finally got my drink.

We here in Israel are spoiled. Israeli hotels – at least the ones that are kosher, and they are the vast majority – make provisions for Sabbath-observant guests. There are special Shabbat elevators that automatically stop on each floor. Even the hotels that use electronic key cards offer their guests the option on Friday afternoon of switching to old-fashioned metal keys.

The strangest Shabbat challenge I have ever experienced was in

Hiroshima, Japan. I was on the 11th floor, which in itself was a challenge, and I had an electronic key. But, somehow, I worked all of that out. The biggest problem was the toilet. It was a highly sophisticated model, such that just moving close to it activated certain sensors. Every time I needed to go to the toilet, just by moving in that direction, I would be violating the Shabbat. On the other hand, I realized that there was no way I could go for twenty-four hours without using the toilet. Since I had no rabbi there with whom to consult, I made my own Halakhic decision: my purpose in nearing the toilet was certainly not to activate any sensors. That was a completely unintended by-product of my actions. I decided to use the toilet as much as I needed and, upon my return to Jerusalem, consult with a rabbi.

When I came home, I spoke with a young rabbi who's a friend from our congregation. He assured me that I had done the only thing I could have. I can only assume that as technology advances around the world, there will be more and more challenges for travelers who keep the Shabbat.

But we shouldn't focus only on the prohibitions of the Shabbat. These might make for some amusing stories, but the main point of the Shabbat is the opportunity to rest, relax, celebrate, contemplate and meditate, read, converse, worship, enjoy, go for a leisurely walk, spend "quality time" with others or with ourselves. I often feel strange about the use of the word "retreat" to refer to a time of study, reflection and prayer – I would hope that a more appropriate term would be "advance." Shabbat for me is a weekly opportunity to experience this advance or, as I quoted earlier, the "weekly exercise in profound living."

Rabbi David Rosen is one of the most prominent Jews in international, inter-religious circles. I once had the privilege of being with him in the Vatican, for an audience with Pope Benedict XVI. He is a Modern Orthodox rabbi who studied in one of the important ultra-Orthodox *Yeshivot*. Still, in the Vatican, he was like a fish in water. I was very impressed.

In 1999, David and I were invited to attend a meeting at the Israeli Ministry of Education. I thought that the meeting was about the forthcoming trip to Israel on the part of the then-Pope, John Paul II, which had been planned for 2000. It was hoped that hundreds of thousands of Christian Pilgrims would follow him and celebrate the new millennium in the Holy Land. It was my understanding that the Ministry had called us in to explore educational ways of preparing Israeli Jewish schoolchildren for this important development.

I came to the meeting well-prepared with a list of ideas for educational activities, speakers, films, site visits for class trips, how the units could be integrated into various aspects of the school curricula, etc. To my dismay, the chairman of the meeting began by asking why, in view of the Crusades and the Inquisition, we should welcome all these Christians!

The rest, of course, is history. John Paul II did come for a historic visit, in the spring. But then, Ariel Sharon went up on the Temple Mount in September and the Second Intifada broke out. The deluge of millennial tourists didn't happen, although Jerusalem has since become a requisite site for future Papal visits. A year later was Sept. 11, 2001.

That, too, is an important personal story. The Lutheran World Federation, together with the World Council of Churches, sponsored a Lutheran-Jewish consultation, looking at antisemitism and anti-Judaism in the Gospels, the writings of Martin Luther and the Holocaust. The structure of the conference would be that each of twenty or so countries would send one Jew and one Lutheran, with the German Churches represented more prominently. There were several observers from outside the Lutheran Church, including Roman Catholics and at least one Orthodox Christian. The Inter-Religious Coordinating Council in Israel sent me to represent Israel. I was supposed to have a Palestinian interlocutor, the Rev. Mitri Raheb of Bethlehem, whom I knew from Seoul in 1990, but in the end, he couldn't come.

The conference was held at a beautiful Catholic retreat center in the woods just outside of Budapest, at the Danube Bend. The area had the almost-unpronounceable name of Dobogoko. The days of the conference: September 9–13.

The first half of the conference was devoted to reports from the various countries, as well as a first-hand report from two people who had just returned from the so-called Conference against Racism in Durban from August 31st to September 8th. That meeting had turned into a platform for vehemently anti-Israel sentiment.

The material from our meeting has been documented in a booklet called *A Shift in Jewish-Lutheran Relations?* published in 2003 by the LWF. During the morning of the 11th, people from a number of countries were invited to wrap up, with me being designated as the last speaker before the lunch break. I used the opportunity to mention a relatively new form of terrorism that had been seen just the day before in Istanbul – suicide bombers. Three Turkish policemen had been killed by a suicide bomber. Perhaps some people felt that I was being an alarmist.

After the break, at around 3 p.m., we split into smaller discussion groups. The leader of our group was a Russian Orthodox priest, based in England. As we were getting settled in our seats, I noticed a Jew from Munich going in and out of our room, talking nervously on his cell phone. I still have a pretty negative attitude to cell phones, but then I found them really annoying. What could possibly be so important that he would make it difficult for us to begin our session?

The leader of our group asked, "What can we as Christians and Jews do together to promote peace and justice?" At that moment, the German Jew rushed in and said, "I'm sorry; we have to stop our discussion – the US has just been attacked." Of course, all the groups stopped. The problem in our retreat center was that there was only one television. It was hard for all of us to gather around it, to watch the news unfold. To this day, there are two iconic images that I never saw in real time – the attack on the Twin Towers in 2001 and the tsunami in December, 2004. During the latter event, I was at a LIMMUD conference in England, at which I think there was no television at all.

Rather than just watching the awful events of September 11th on TV, many of the people at our interfaith gathering tried to contact relatives and friends in New York, but they couldn't get through. For the second half of our conference, we shifted our focus to current events. On the night of the 11th, we held an inter-religious memorial service for the victims of that day's tragedy, inviting local churches to participate. The only individual about whom I was worried was my cousin Jay, who works in Lower Manhattan, but not as low as the World Trade Center. It turned out that he indeed had to walk home to Long Island that day.

My personal worry was a rather silly one, yet enough to cause minor anxiety. There were no planes flying right after Sept. 11th, and I felt I had to get home for the weekend, which would be followed a day or so later by Rosh Hashanah. I pictured myself getting stranded in Europe. It reminded me of Herman Wouk's book, *War & Remembrance*, in which a young American Jewish woman, Natalie Jastrow, is trapped in Europe and ends up in a concentration camp! After several moments of reflecting on that horrific thought, I realized that I have friends in different parts of Europe and, if necessary, I can travel to them by train for the holiday. That of course made me feel much better. What made me feel best was that the planes started flying again and I got home, safe and sound, just in time to celebrate the New Year in Jerusalem.

The most important part of this experience for me was that many of the people I met at that conference have become quite significant in my life since then as friends and colleagues. I guess we share a deep bond. The Jew from Munich served as Treasurer of the ICCJ when I was President. One of the other Jews I met there was Rabbi Abraham Skorka, a close friend and confidant of Pope Francis. And I met several Christians who became close friends of mine.

In 2011, I was invited to Paris to mark forty years of dialogue between the Vatican and the Jewish people. My hotel was in the center of Paris (L'Etoile) and my room was on the 17th floor. Never before or since have I been pampered with such a view. But the whole week was an experience of being pampered. The entire conference was strictly kosher-catered. We had fine wine and whiskey, veal, duck, delicious desserts. The last night of the meeting, we all took a boat trip around the beautifully and dramatically illuminated city of Paris. Again, all the food and drinks were kosher. As we got on board, there was a band playing Klezmer music. After a while, they started playing world music and then answered any requests we had. Before the dessert, we got up to dance. A representative of the Vatican whom I knew as someone who likes to enjoy himself got into the dancing. He sat on a chair and we lifted him into the air, as if he were a Bar Mitzvah boy or a groom. Thus, inter-religious dialogue can be serious and important but also, a lot of fun.

Israel Independence Day in New Zealand

I SPENT THE YEAR OF 2003–2004 in Australia. I was on Sabbatical, and it was the best year of my life. Although that entire year, I didn't attend a wedding, I also didn't attend a funeral or pay a shiva call. That was because for one year, I was living on the margins of a community, but not really in it. The best thing about that year may have been that I also didn't attend any meetings. Before the Sabbatical, I had been in Australia twice and since, four more times. I love almost everything Australian and after Jerusalem, my second favorite city in the world is Sydney.

During the Sabbatical, I decided to visit New Zealand for the first time. I had a two-week break from my teaching in Sydney just after Pesach. Although it would mean being by myself for Shoah (Holocaust) Remembrance Day, Israeli Remembrance Day and Israel Independence Day, I decided to take advantage of the opportunity and have a real sight-seeing vacation. I was in New Zealand for two Shabbatot; the first, in Auckland, the second, in Wellington. The communities welcomed me. I "sang for my supper"; in Auckland, I spoke at a communal Shabbat lunch and in Wellington, as I noted before, I spoke at a communal Friday night dinner. In between, I had a week on the North Island and almost a week on the South Island. It's a very beautiful and interesting country.

For the Israeli national remembrance days, I found appropriate things to do. The Memorial Museum in Auckland had a corner devoted to the Shoah; the big national museum in Wellington, *Te Papa*, had a war memorial exhibit; I lit memorial candles in my hotel rooms. But the challenge was greater on Israel Independence Day – I'm used to a whole country celebrating with me. In addition to reciting the appropriate prayers, I symbolically dressed in blue-and-white, the colors of our flag. I knew it was unlikely that anyone else would notice, but at least I was reminding myself that the day was special.

That morning, I went on a tour to Mt. Cook and joked to myself that it was a shame it wasn't named for the great Religious Zionist thinker, Rabbi Kook. In the morning, on the way up, we had stopped on the main – or, maybe, only – street in a little town, where there was a souvenir shop and I got a cup of coffee. In the afternoon, coming down, we stopped at the exact same place. I love variety and I found this repetitive and thus even a bit boring. I decided to leave the group for a while, strike out on my own, and see what different stores might be on the other side of the street.

Something caught my eye. A man in a *kippa* was standing on the other side of the street, talking on a cell phone. Without hearing a word he was saying, I knew he must be Israeli. I walked over to him, tapped him on the shoulder, and said, "*Chag Sameach* (happy holiday)." He smiled broadly and called over his wife and the other couple with whom they were traveling. We chatted in Hebrew for a few minutes – they were from Jerusalem, and we knew certain people in common. I realized that I had to go back to my group, but not without thanking them for having "made my day."

Then I realized something else – there were two reasons to account for this pleasant surprise: the fact that I noticed his *kippa* was surely one of them. But the other was that I had acted independently by leaving the group. Perhaps these two things sum up my vision of Israel: an independent state that is both Jewish and democratic.

Ezekiel and Hiroshima

I N 2008, I ATTENDED an inter-religious conference in Hiroshima. One of the speakers was the Reverend Dr. Bill Vendley, head of an international organization called Religions for Peace. He suggested that we would do well to listen to the accumulated wisdom within the various religious traditions. After all, the religions of the world have been around, in some cases, for thousands of years and, in other cases, for "only" hundreds of years, but that's a long time, too. In that time, they have all had deep conversations about two basic questions: (1) What does it mean to live a good life as a human being? (2) What does it mean to live in community?

Regarding the question of what it means to live a good life, the biblical book of Psalms has a wise answer in Psalm 34:13–14 (my translation): "Who is it who desires life, loves days, that he may see good therein; keep your tongue from evil, etc. " Most readers interpret "loves days" as part of the question, "Who desires life?" According to that approach, the answer begins with "keep your tongue from evil and your lips from speaking guile."

But I would like to suggest an alternate understanding of the verse, in which "loving days" and "seeing good" are already part of the answer. Living and loving the day. A habit I adopted several years ago – each day, before I go to sleep, I ask myself, "What good things happened today?" Later, when I took a course in mindfulness-based stress reduction, I learned that recording daily at least three things for which I am grateful is a helpful practice. Writing them down, apparently, is even more effective for stress reduction than just thinking about them.

Similarly, in Ecclesiastes 3:13," That everyone may eat and drink, and find satisfaction in all his toil – this is the gift of God." (New International Version) It is a gift to be able to find satisfaction and to see the good. But we can work on ourselves to develop that gift. And to recognize that sometimes, answers may be hidden in our questions themselves.

I found that the city of Hiroshima itself is a testament to human resilience and desire for life. It is a large and bustling city which has at its heart an interesting museum and a moving memorial, commemorating the staggering tragedy. At the conference at which Dr. Vendley spoke, we concluded with a multi-faith ceremony involving the Hiroshima Memorial.

There were ten different religious groups represented (true, four of them were variations on the Shinto tradition). Each group, in turn, took a few minutes to pray or perform a ritual, often in its own language – Japanese, Arabic, etc. We then marched out together in silence and placed flowers on the Memorial. I was just a trifle disappointed that the Jewish contribution was all in English – not a word of Hebrew – but the content was powerful. An Israeli woman named Dahlia read – in English – Ezekiel's vision of the valley of dry bones (37:1–14). It was uncannily appropriate for the setting.

Later that evening, I had a drink with a Norwegian journalist who was perhaps one of the most secular people I have ever met. He asked, "That beautiful passage that Dahlia read today – did she write it?" I actually felt sorry for him. He had been robbed of part of his heritage as a cultured Western person.

I have to insert here that I have an ambivalent relationship with the media and with journalists. (Perhaps this goes back to my experience with the women's magazine when I was 17.) I can, literally, state that "some of my best friends are journalists." On the other hand, I had an unsuccessful work experience with them in the late 1990s. I was working at the Van Leer Institute, a prestigious Jerusalem-based institution for engaged research and educational projects dealing with the important issues of the day. I wanted to run a series of encounters/conversations between educators and journalists, under the rubric of "The Educational *Responsibility* of the Media." The participating journalists all objected to the title, saying they felt no educational responsibility. They suggested as an alternative, "The Educational *Influence* of the Media." I acquiesced.

Author at her desk, 1994

The sessions were poorly attended; quite a few of the educators came regularly; the journalists came only when they were asked in advance to speak, but not to listen to others.

It isn't only journalists who are ignorant about dialogue. In 2006, I was invited to attend a conference in Antalya, Turkey. At the Ben-Gurion Airport outside of Tel-Aviv, a young Israeli security man was checking through my luggage. He asked me why I'm going to Turkey. I answered, "For a conference." He then asked, "What is the conference about?" I replied, "Inter-religious dialogue." And he said, "There is no such thing!"

The beautiful passage in Ezekiel has played at least two more roles in my life. First, every time I bring a group of Christians to a visit to Yad Vashem, we read it before we go, as the fourteenth verse is engraved on the gate. Some Jews see it as a prophecy that has been fulfilled in the State of Israel. In the eleventh verse of the passage, the bones rise up and say "Our hope is lost." I mentioned earlier in the memoir that "*HaTikvah*" – the hope – is our national anthem; the author of that anthem, 19th century Russian-Jewish poet Naftali Hertz Imber, wrote: "Our hope is not yet lost."

But, second, in the very early 90s when the Soviet Empire broke up, I had the privilege – and challenge – of teaching a small group of Jewish educators from the FSU who had come to study at the Hebrew University. They came from Kharkov and Vitebsk, Riga and Moscow, and elsewhere. I was impressed with their high level of Hebrew, especially in so far as it contrasted with their almost total lack of Jewish knowledge and experience. I taught a class on Jewish festivals and when I asked if they had any childhood memories of the festivals, the woman from Riga mentioned a grandmother who had occasionally lit candles and had baked little triangular cakes (which turned out to be *Hamentaschen*, for Purim.) But no one else had any memories. They appreciated any new information I could give them.

One day, we opened our Bibles to Ezekiel 37. I read it aloud in Hebrew, while they followed along in the Russian translation. When I finished, there was total silence in the room, for what seemed like a long time. Finally, the man from Vitebsk said, "That is our story."

Younan

ONE OF MY FRIENDS in Jerusalem is Bishop Munib Younan, the Palestinian Lutheran Bishop of Jerusalem. Whenever I despair – and that is much of the time – Munib reminds me, "As long as you believe in a Living God, you must have hope." In February of 2013, the ICCJ Board issued a statement about the Israeli-Palestinian conflict, using that as our motto.

Munib and I were together in Thessaloniki in 1996, at a conference on "The Future of Jerusalem" with Jews, Christians and Muslims. Thessaloniki (also known as Salonica) used to be called by Jews "the Jerusalem of Greece." It had a large Jewish community which sometimes reached more than half of the total population. Many of the Jewish men worked in the harbor and, because they were, by and large, traditional, the harbor had to close on the Sabbath and Jewish festivals. Up to 97% of the Jewish community was murdered during the Holocaust. When we organized for the conference participants a special tour of Jewish Thessaloniki, Munib was one of the only Palestinians who joined the tour and took part in the ceremony at the Holocaust memorial.

In 2013, I participated in a workshop with Israeli and American Jews, European and Palestinian Christians. Bishop Munib, who by now had been elected President of the Lutheran World Federation, convened the workshop. Our theme was the liberating aspects of the Exodus story and their implications for our particular context. One morning, we piled into a minibus for a field trip. We went to Ramallah. I hadn't been there in years. It's a modern, bustling city, which might be able to serve as a model for further development on the West Bank. Most of our morning was spent visiting a Church-sponsored school, where the kids sang and danced for us. I had a good feeling about the school.

Before going back to Jerusalem, some of the Palestinian members of our group suggested that we should visit Yasser Arafat's grave. I wasn't too keen on that but, being the only Jew on the bus, I went along with it. Of course, as several people pointed out, the grave was empty, since Arafat's body had been exhumed to investigate allegations of foul play leading to his death.

This was, I believe, a Wednesday. I was expecting company for Friday night dinner and so, that evening, I made gefilte fish. Then I started thinking about what an interesting life I lead. How many people can say that in the same day, they both visited Arafat's grave *and* made gefilte fish? And if there are such people, it's likely that I know them!

In a slightly more serious vein, I think that making gefilte fish symbolizes for me doing something that is very particularistically Jewish. It can be integrated with inter-religious and inter-cultural dialogue, which I perceive as an expression of universal values. I returned for further sessions of the Bishop's dialogue workshop, in 2014 and in 2015. The themes, respectively, were "Use of Land and Water" and "Be Prophetic!"

From Porto Alegre
to Heidelberg

F OR SEVEN YEARS, BEGINNING IN 2002, I was privileged to
be part of the WCC think tank, which I mentioned earlier.
The group was initiated by the man who was then in charge
of inter-religious dialogue for the WCC, the Revd. Dr. Hans Ucko,
a Swedish Lutheran with Jewish roots. In February 2006, in Porto
Alegre, Brazil, at the WCC Assembly, Hans chaired a panel discussion with members of the group on what we have learned through
the process of our encounters. Buddhist scholar Rita Gross made
the point – I think she was actually quoting Professor Diana Eck of
Harvard – that to know only one religion is to know none. In other
words, the comparative perspective sheds light and gives deeper
insights into our own faith traditions.

Coincidentally, the very next day was Shabbat and I was walking down
the street with the wife of the Habad rabbi of Porto Alegre. She spoke
about the challenge of raising her children in five different languages.
I'm guessing that the five are English, Hebrew, Yiddish, Portuguese and
Spanish. This Orthodox woman made the point that once you know a
second or third language, you also know your own language better, as
you acquire comparative insights into, for example, grammar and syntax.

I believe that this phenomenon applies as well to interpretations of
religious texts. When I introduce a seminar on Jewish texts, especially
for a Gentile group, I often begin with a humorous and slightly irrev-
erent story:

I assume that God looks at the earth every day. But on this particular
day, the Holy One, Blessed be He, looked down to see how Jews were

behaving. Jews are human beings and, therefore, they sin, they make mistakes and foolish choices. Jews are no better than anyone else. I would add, parenthetically, that I also believe that we're no worse.

God saw some Jews lying, stealing, cheating, or – Heaven forbid – doing even worse sins. He said, "Oh, my God," or whatever God would say on such an occasion: "I'm going to take back my *Torah*; you're not living by it, anyway."

So, first, there came rolling back to Heaven all the scrolls of the Torah, the Pentateuch, from all the different synagogues in the world. But then came all the commentaries on the Torah, and all the poetry written on the commentaries, and the commentaries written on the poetry; the rest of the books of the Bible, and the commentaries on them; the corpus of rabbinic Midrash, and all the commentaries on it; the legal commentary called the Mishnah, and all the commentaries on the Mishnah, the most famous one being the Talmud, and all the commentaries on the Talmud. There are actually two Talmuds, one from Babylonia and one from the land of Israel, and they each have their own commentaries, and they in turn have commentaries upon the commentaries. Then, at some point in the early Middle Ages, some folks said, "there's so much 'stuff' out there; let's at least codify the legal material." So, various rabbis compiled legal codes, but others came along and wrote commentaries on the codes. Then, some said (and sometimes it was even the same people), "the way to 'make sense' of all this stuff" is through rational philosophy, and they wrote philosophies of Torah, but others came along and wrote commentaries upon the philosophy. The more mystically minded wrote mystical commentaries, including the *Zohar*, which formed the basis for Kabbalah, or Jewish mysticism, and then others wrote commentaries on the *Zohar*. To make a very long story just a trifle shorter, we'll skip whole genres and by this time, as you can guess, all the commentaries on them . . . Anyway, by now, Heaven was completely overflowing, and God said, "Take back my Torah; you've earned the right to keep it."[1]

I appreciate that the story doesn't try to portray Jews as any better than we are. But it does emphasize the central role that texts have played in our culture. Unfortunately, one of the things that is most appealing

---

1. Despite my attempts, I have been unable to locate the source of this story. It seems unlikely that I simply made it up.

to me about Jewish culture is also highly problematic for many other Jews. I love our intellectual traditions, our texts and their commentaries. The intellectual challenge is one of the main things that attract me to traditional Judaism. Yet many, if not most Jews today, especially in the Diaspora, are not sufficiently knowledgeable to feel comfortable within traditional Jewish culture. They lack the minimal linguistic and textual skills to feel "at home." Rather than watering down Judaism, I believe the solution is emphasizing Jewish education for children, young people and adults. Before my retirement in 2009, I devoted over forty years of my career to Jewish education throughout the world.

In June 2014 I was in Heidelberg, Germany just for a few days, for a meeting of a working group of Christians and Jews from the ICCJ. The project deals with "Promise, Land and Hope," and is meant to help people make sense of the many opposing positions on the Arab-Israel conflict. We generally have an annual meeting in a different venue in the U.S., Europe or Israel. In this case, we met at the "Hochshule" – a kind of academy for advanced Jewish study that's connected with the University in Heidelberg. They have about 150 students, including masters and Ph.D. students, and ten regular faculty. Most of them aren't Jewish. They also bring additional faculty from Israel and other places. A secondary story before the main one: When I arrived, I was warmly received by a tall young woman – a German non-Jew – who told me, "You were my teacher at the Hebrew University in 1985." Of course, I didn't remember her, but she remembered me, and she now heads the Department of Jewish History.

Heidelberg, in the Middle Ages, was an important Jewish community. In 1938, the community was seriously hurt by the events of Krystall-nacht, or what some people call the "Reichspogrom," and for several decades, there was little Jewish life to speak of. The Hochshule was founded in 1979.

We were offered a tour that included a visit to the library. There, I became aware of the "Heidelberg Talmud." This is a special edition of the Talmud that was published in Heidelberg in 1948, by the U.S. Army Chaplains and the American Jewish Joint Distribution Committee. Two Lithuanian rabbis from the *Slobodka Mussar Yeshiva* wrote the dedication and expressed great appreciation to the publishers. They must have used this Talmud in a Displaced Persons' camp. They wrote that the only chance for continuing Jewish life in Europe is through Jewish education and the study of Torah. I would add that I think that's the only chance anywhere.

Most editions of the Talmud do not feature illustrations. But sometimes, there is a frontispiece. To the extent that it has pictures, they are usually of a Holy Ark in a synagogue or, perhaps, an artist's conception of what the Temple might have looked like. On the frontispiece of this volume, however, there were a few drawings: at the bottom of the page, drawings of barbed wire and a concentration camp; going up along the sides, palm trees; at the top, a drawing of the Land of Israel. And this was in 1948! I felt myself as an Israeli Jew deeply moved by the experience of seeing this in Heidelberg.

About two weeks after this incident, the Gaza War (euphemistically called "Operation Protective Edge") broke out. Several times during the fighting, I thought back to the story in Heidelberg. It helped.

In what way did it help?

Israel found itself in an impossible situation in 2014, partially, I would suggest, of our own making. We were becoming increasingly isolated, at the same time that parts of our country were under almost constant rocket barrage from Gaza. We were horrified by the abduction and murder of three teenagers. The proverbial straw that broke the camel's back was the discovery of the tunnels leading from Gaza into our territory. At the time, I knew someone who lived on a kibbutz in that area. Far from a right-winger, she was justifiably concerned with the safety of her family. And scared to death.

But at the same time, many of us felt sincere concern for the Palestinians in Gaza. We were mourning their innocent losses, together with our own.

Even under "good" conditions – to the extent that there have been any – most of the Gazans live in abject squalor. One of our problems is that both the Israelis and the Palestinians see themselves as the victims of the conflict. They seem to be competitors in what I call a "suffering sweepstakes." One of the problems with victimhood is that it prevents the victim from assuming responsibility for his or her actions, including the victimization of others. In the Israeli-Palestinian conflict, I believe that both sides are victims and both sides are victimizers. I really think that the least helpful thing people can do – and regrettably, many well-meaning people do this – is to portray the situation in terms of a zero-sum game, in which, if you're pro-Palestinian, you must be anti-

the Heidelberg Talmud, photo
by Brad Seligmann

Israeli, and vice versa. We must be *both* pro-Palestinian *and* pro-Israeli, because we're pro-people and, therefore, pro-peace.

During the fighting in Gaza, there was rioting, tensions and hostility directed by our extreme right at the left and the Israeli Arabs, and racist incitement. Much of it took place on the social media networks, which, thankfully, I'm not part of. At the time, many Jews spoke of a wonderful feeling of unity in our country, but I didn't really identify with that. It didn't extend to Israeli Arabs.

Remembering the Heidelberg Talmud helped me keep some valuable perspective on a very bad situation. Without neglecting the central role of the land of Israel in Judaism, I focused on the continuity of Jewish history through Torah. The commandment most often repeated in the Torah (it appears no less than thirty-six times) is "Do not oppress the stranger, for you were strangers in the land of Egypt." Justice and peace are religious values no less than the sanctity of the land of Israel.

The year since "Protective Edge" has seen the continuing rise of Jewish fundamentalism and extremism. At a demonstration protesting the arson attempt at Jerusalem's Bi-lingual School in November, I had a raw egg thrown at me – for the first time in about fifty years of attending demonstrations. It would appear that Jewish extremists attacked the Church of the Loaves and Fishes in the Galilee in June, and burned down a Palestinian home, killing a baby and both his parents in July of 2015. People who try to defend the Israeli Supreme Court and the rule of law – and who themselves are right-wingers – are sometimes stigmatized as "left-wing radicals." I don't know how all of this will end.

More on Food

I HAVEN'T ALWAYS KEPT KOSHER. I grew up in a deeply Jewish, but non-religious, home. My Yiddish-speaking grandmother, Bobbie Ina, who lived with us, served bacon and French fries for lunch. When I was about six years old, I caused great embarrassment to my parents. We were invited out for dinner to the home of some people who were quite religious. They must have served cold cuts, because I asked them, "May I have some more ham, please?"

This story fits in with two others, not related to food, which I remember – probably because my parents told me, rather than because I actually remember them. Once, when I was about six, they took me to F.A.O. Schwarz, on Fifth Avenue. They explained to me that it's the world's biggest and best toy store, but that many things in the store were simply beyond our means. They did say they would buy one toy for me. The truth is, I remember, perhaps from a later visit to the store, that there were stuffed animals going for thousands of dollars. Anyway, I apparently ran through the store, shouting at the top of my lungs: "Can we afford this? Can we afford that?"

Similarly, when I was about the same age, they took me to what they said would be a concert. The evening began with a series of long, tedious speeches. I blurted, in a loud voice: "You said we were going to a concert – this is just a boring meeting!"

I began to keep kosher when we moved from Akron to Haverhill, in 1960. I was about thirteen at the time and very adolescent. Haverhill was the smallest Jewish community we had ever lived in. My father felt that as someone employed by the community he should support its institutions, including the kosher butcher. So when we moved to Haverhill, we started buying kosher meat, although we still ate meat and dairy together, and certainly didn't separate utensils. I thought that it was hypocritical to eat kosher meat at home but not outside, so I started eating only kosher meat, all the time. Giving up bacon was difficult. I still remember the taste of shrimp, but I think that I had eaten relatively little shellfish all along. I remember that during high school, when I went out with my friends, I mostly ate tuna fish salad sandwiches.

During my college years, I decided to become stricter in my practice. From the age of about 21, I have not eaten food that was cooked in non-kosher settings. In a non-kosher home or restaurant, I do allow myself to eat cold salads. My parents' home became a little stricter; by the time they moved to Riverdale, they were using separate sets of dishes, pots, cutlery, and so on – but they did not keep any dietary laws outside of their home. I remember once my parents and I went out to dinner in New York. We went to a non-kosher restaurant. My father ordered beef Stroganoff, my mother had shrimp cocktail, and I ate a fruit salad. After that evening, I asked if, at least in a place like New York, we could try to go to kosher restaurants from then on. They agreed.

I have found in general that non-Jews are respectful of my dietary practices. Once, in 1973, I planned a week's visit to Denmark. I had a Danish student at the time – not Jewish – whom I told about my plans. She gave me the phone number of her sister, who lives outside Copenhagen, suggesting I should call there when I arrive.

The sister seemed happy to hear from me and invited me to take the train and visit them Sunday afternoon. It was only when I was already on the train that I realized that Sunday afternoon must have meant dinner, and that I hadn't alerted them to my quirks. Soon after I arrived, my hostess said, "We usually have meat for dinner, but since you're from Israel, I thought you might not be able to eat our meat. So I went out and got you shrimp."

I replied, "That is very kind of you, but actually, I can't eat shrimp, either." She was very gracious and said, "Come into the kitchen, open the refrigerator and tell me what you *can* eat." Among the fresh fruits and vegetables, dairy products and so on, we put together a very good meal. But I learned from that incident never to assume anything and always to let people know. Also, whenever I invite people to my home for a meal, I ask what they can and cannot eat.

I have never been tempted to go vegetarian or certainly not vegan – more on that later – perhaps because I experience keeping kosher as already quite limiting. I mentioned earlier that Rabbi Yitz Greenberg has been a role model. He recognizes the importance of being able to go out with your family and friends, even if it means entering a non-kosher restaurant. I should note that some rabbis would forbid such an act, partly because people who saw you might think you were going to eat something you shouldn't. Yitz said we should ask, "Now, what *can* I eat in this place?" And if all you can have is a Coke, order the Coke and sit and drink it with your friends.

In the last few years, some of my friends who used to eat red meat have given it up and stayed only with poultry; some who used to eat poultry now eat only fish; some pescatarians have become lacto-ovo vegetarians; and some vegetarians have become vegans. Veganism has become quite trendy in Israel, especially in Tel-Aviv. A friend of mine told me that Israel is the fastest-growing vegan country in the world. I know the arguments for it and there are many articles in the weekend newspapers touting the merits of being a vegan. In the land of milk and honey, some secular Israelis who used to scorn people who kept the Jewish dietary laws, now eschew honey and milk, because they are animal products.[1]

There was a man who used to be in our community who was the first vegan I ever knew. He once said something cute: He was asked if he's a vegan for health reasons or ethical reasons and he replied, "Health reasons; the health of the animals." Now, I must indicate that I don't hate animals. I'm not allergic to cats or dogs and sometimes I even enjoy playing with them in other people's houses. The Jewish tradition mandates a respect for life and a prohibition against cruelty to animals. But, if I could think of a way in which to become even more carnivorous, I would do so, as a kind of backlash. (Perhaps I could become a cannibal?!)

Why is this so important to me? I admit that it's partly because I like meat. But it's a lot more than just that. My basic belief system is rooted in the notion that all human beings are equally created in the image of God. This belief enables religious people to embrace human rights and to cooperate with secular humanists.

But the secular world is changing. For example, in some of the pro-

1. I do know that the Biblical honey comes from dates, but that would ruin the point.

gressive countries of Europe – e.g., Denmark in 2013 – parliaments have legislated a ban on *shehita*, the kosher slaughter of animals. This is done in the name of animal rights. In effect, animal rights have been given priority over the human right of freedom of religion. I suppose that humanism, secular or religious, is one of the "grand narratives" rejected by post-modernists. I'm a modern person living in a post-modern world, and it's very hard.

My friends know me as a neo-Luddite. I'm always one of the last people, if at all, to purchase a new machine or gadget. I don't have a Smartphone and I don't get involved with social media. I still think of text as a noun, not a verb. Some of this is for economic reasons, but some is also ideological. When I see young people who have itchy thumbs from "texting," it reminds me of the famous scene in the film "Modern Times" when Charlie Chaplin leaves the factory, but is still making the involuntary motions of his work on the assembly line.

The challenge or perhaps threat to the central role of human beings is not only from the side of animal rights. It's also from the development of artificial intelligence and machines. I used to think that was only in science fiction films, but then I learned about a new phenomenon called Transhumanism, which is an international movement with the goal of developing and making widely available technologies to greatly enhance human intellectual, physical, and psychological capacities. Transhumanist thinkers emphasize the potential benefits of emerging technologies that could overcome fundamental human limitations. They speculate that human beings may eventually be able to transform themselves into beings with such greatly expanded abilities as to merit the label "post human." I assume that just as in our world, excellent medical care is often available only to people with the means to pay for it, in the future, we may have two races emerging – the post humans who can afford all of the technological supplements, and the rest of humanity, who can't. A truly frightening thought.

I believe in a hierarchy within nature. I suppose that this belief, which jibes with the evolutionary biological scale, opens me – a strong opponent of racism and sexism – to the accusation of "speciesism." Then so be it. We are, as Jewish tradition tells us, both the crown of creation and mortal, finite creatures.

A few years ago, there was an air travel crisis in Europe, due to the eruption of an obscure volcano in Iceland. It was an extremely difficult time for many, causing personal hardship (such as missed weddings and funerals) or economic losses. Yet, as a religious person, I looked at it in a different way: we have become all too used to the idea that natural disasters occur only in faraway places like Haiti or Nepal. The fact that for several days, air travel in the heartland of Europe, with all its technological advancement, was paralyzed, shows us that human beings are still limited creatures, very much at the mercy of nature. (The Hebrew phrase that comes to mind is "the mercy of Heaven," double entendre very much intended here.)

We must never lose sight of our finitude. This should have been a humbling experience for us all, showing us how much we have in common with our fellow human beings throughout the world. The 20th century French Jewish philosopher Emanuel Levinas taught us to see God in the face of the Other. I don't remember where I heard the following, but someone once said that's a pretty tall order; it would be enough if we could just look at the Other and see a face no less human than our own.

Visit to Bosnia

I N THE SUMMER OF 2006, I joined an inter-religious study trip to Bosnia. I was the only Jew among the sixteen participants, although there were two more Jews on the staff. The others were Christians and Muslims from quite a few countries, including several places in the former Soviet Central Asian republics, from which I had never met anyone before.

When you ride into Sarajevo from the airport, you see many buildings full of bullet holes. But my main memory of the city is a magical evening that we spent at a restaurant outside, in the hills, with the city lights and the stars in seeming competition with each other. Almost nine years later, I saw Kusturica's film, "Life is a Miracle," which corroborated my initial impression of Sarajevo.

Part of our experience of being in Bosnia involved living in the homes of Muslim families in a small, picturesque town called Stolac. I stayed with a young family in which an uncle had been killed in the not-so-long-before War. They were wonderful to me, respecting my dietary needs and strange customs. We arrived there one day before *Tisha B'Av*, the 9th of Av, a fast day in the summer that commemorates the destruction of both Temples in Jerusalem. I explained to the group and to my hosts that for a full 25-hour period, from sunset to nightfall the next day, I would not be able to eat or drink. My hosts were not devout Muslims, but they were partially observant and certainly understood the concept of a dawn-to-dusk fast.

The leader of our group in Bosnia was an-otherwise observant Jew who idiosyncratically did not mark the 9th of Av. He thought that the destruction of the Temple and the beginning of Jewish Exile were good things, so he saw no reason to fast on that day. On the evening of the 9th of Av, when it is customary to chant the Book of Lamentations in the synagogue in a mournful atmosphere, he took the rest of our group out to dinner in a restaurant. I chose not to join them, but to stay behind and do the ritual for *Tisha B'Av*, by myself.

I asked permission to use the *maktab* for my private prayers and chanting. The *maktab*, from the Semitic root for "writing," is an annex to the mosque. If it were adjacent to a synagogue, I would call it the *Beit Midrash*, or study hall. It was not in use that evening, and the community readily agreed. I chose that spot for two practical reasons and one spiritual one. First, it was pleasantly air-conditioned. Second, the custom on the 9th of Av is to sit on the floor or on low benches, as do mourners. In the *maktab*, one always sat on pillows or low sofas. The spiritual reason is that I believe that Islam is a monotheistic faith, dedicated to the One God whom I worship, as well.

I said my evening prayers and intoned the Book of Lamentations to myself. It was strange, because for as long as I can remember, I have been with some type of Jewish community for the 9th of Av, whether in a synagogue or a summer camp. There, I was alone, and it felt a bit lonely. The moment I completed the reading – probably about 10 p.m. – the *muezzin* began his call to the faithful to go to the mosque for their evening prayers. But suddenly I realized something that made the entire experience meaningful for me: I had just read a lament for the destroyed city of Jerusalem, which I have been privileged to see being rebuilt. Stolac was a town destroyed by war, now being rebuilt. Destruction and rebuilding, one of the major themes of the 9th of Av, was right there, before my eyes.

Another story from this trip to Bosnia relates to how I see the role of dialogue. There's a lot of talk in inter-religious and inter-cultural circles about how dialogue and education aren't enough; we need activism. I don't share that view; I think that dialogue and education are forms of activism. In Bosnia, another member of our program was an Arab Israeli, who didn't especially identify with any faith, but had been raised as a "cultural" Christian. We shared Hebrew as a common language. I had met her in passing before the program, but we didn't really know each other until our experience together in Bosnia.

One day, all the members of our group were mobilized into doing work projects in Stolac. She and I were supposed to paint the wall of a room in a building that was being fixed up to serve as a youth center. We spent a couple of hours together and had a really interesting conversation. I'm not much of a painter, and I have a feeling that someone will have to go over the paint job I did before the building is usable. But our working together provided the setting for a good dialogue.

Names

IN THE SUMMER OF 2013, I attended the annual ICCJ conference that we held in Aix-en-Provence, in the south of France. Very nearby is "Camp des Milles," a Nazi internment camp, the only one in France that has been preserved and now serves as a Holocaust museum. There, we had a lecture by a very special person. His name is Father Patrick Desbois and he is known throughout the world as someone who organizes groups of volunteers to journey to Eastern Europe, where they dig and uncover mass graves, particularly in the Ukraine and Belarus. The victims who fell into these pits had been shot by the Nazis in what is sometimes referred to as "the Holocaust by bullets." Desbois himself is a charismatic person who made a strong impression on the conference participants, both the Jews and the Christians. I would like to bring one thought from his lecture:

Father Desbois asked about the Cambodian genocide – does anyone in the audience know the name of a single victim? We all know the name of the tyrant Pol Pot who committed the atrocity. Yet the victims remain anonymous. On the other hand, the whole world knew Anne Frank. Father Desbois praised the Jewish people for memorializing the victims of the Holocaust by collecting and documenting their names. That is the meaning of the Biblical phrase "Yad Vashem," (literally, "a hand and a name") a physical and spiritual monument, which is the name of Israel's official Holocaust memorial institution. And as someone who accompanies groups of Christians on visits to Yad Vashem in Jerusalem,

I can attest to the fact that one of the most important places on their visit is the Hall of Names.

And now, I would like to mention that several years ago, a friend asked me an important and troubling question: What is the significance of all the lists in the Torah, long and sometimes tedious lists of names, in the form of "so-and-so begat so-and-so." I suggested, in a spontaneous and non-scholarly answer, that perhaps there was a desire to emphasize that each individual is a world unto himself or herself, and his/her name is important.

I'd like to develop this idea now and learn something positive from my Christian friends. In my experience, many Christians, when someone dies, thank God for that person's life. They celebrate the gift of the person's life. We know, for example, the custom of the wake. This is a kind of party that is held after the funeral. I'm not suggesting that we Jews should adopt this custom – I'm just saying that we should try to remember our loved ones and celebrate their lives.

Visit to the Ukraine

I N THE LAST FEW years, I have become familiar with the concept of the "bucket list"; a personal wish-list of things you want to accomplish before you die ("kick the bucket"). One of the goals I set for myself was to visit at least fifty different countries of the world. According to my calculations, I have done that – but that's only if you count Northern Ireland as a separate unit. I'm still open to visiting more new places. Anyway, my forty-ninth (or forty-eighth, depending on how you count) country was the Ukraine, which I visited for the first time in April 2013. Although Kiev is a beautiful and impressive city, it wasn't a great visit. I think that on the basis of my experience there, I could have predicted that violence would break out shortly thereafter. Part of it was that I still wasn't well (see Chapter 27) – I had developed shingles and was suffering the aftermath of my twenty-seven-week cold. I actually fell down on the street in Kiev and came away a bit bruised. If I say that the highlights of my visit were Babi Yar and the Czernobyl Museum, that may give you some idea of the nature of the visit.

I was invited by a wealthy Jewish oligarch, who is also a Member of Parliament, to attend an inter-religious conference. I hesitate to use the word "dialogue," because the conference wasn't very dialogical. I know that in some Eastern European settings, "dialogue" is just a series of speeches, one after the other. This was the first time in my experience that a conference was picketed by demonstrators in the street, outside of our hotel. They were holding antisemitic signs and criticizing the Orthodox Patriarch of the Ukraine for engaging in dialogue with Jews and other heretics. The next day, the conference went to the Parliament building, for a meeting with some government officials. The same demonstrators followed us and marched outside the Parliament.

I'll note here that I did have a second experience with anti-dialogue demonstrators, but in a very different context. In November of the same year, I attended the Assembly of the World Council of Churches, held in Bhusan, South Korea. If you're not familiar with Bhusan, I can tell you that I wasn't either, until I got invited there for the Assembly. It's a city of several million people, the second largest in South Korea, after Seoul, and, in my view, far more beautiful. We were there for the foliage season. If there is one thing I miss about living in Israel, it's foliage. Outside the conference center, there were daily demonstrations by some members of the Korean National Council of Churches. They didn't mention dialogue with Jews; what disturbed them was dialogue with Buddhists!

Back in Kiev, the end of my trip was probably the worst part. It was Thursday, and I was scheduled for an evening flight from Kiev to Tel-Aviv. The people waiting for the flight were, largely, Jews and, among them, mostly Israelis. I had arrived at the airport a bit early and was reading a book that had been given to me as a gift, with a lovely dedication. The book is a memoir about a Jewish family that was saved by being hidden in Warsaw during the War. The daughter in the book grew up to be my friend, who lives part of the year in Jerusalem and part of the year in Sweden.

There was a bomb scare in the airport. In all the tumult of the bomb scare, I left the book on a table in the airport lounge. We weren't given any information, but were "herded" out, first onto the tarmac, and then onto buses that took us to a forested area a bit further from the terminal. It was getting dark and frankly, I was scared. I suppose the combination of the buses, the landscape, my recent visit to Babi Yar and the book I was reading about the Holocaust, all combined to create a sense of impending disaster. Taking Jews in the Ukraine into the forest at sundown felt like a frightening proposition.

I also began to think about what would happen if I couldn't get back home for Shabbat. I would have to spend Shabbat in Kiev – where would I stay? I suppose the Habad House would take us in, but there would be many of us who needed Shabbat meals – would they be prepared to handle all of us? I would have to do some laundry before Shabbat.

Thinking about laundry seemed a stark contrast to the prospect of getting shot in the Ukrainian forest.

To understand what happened next, I must give some background. Uman is a city in central Ukraine. Since 1811, Jews have been going on pilgrimage to visit the grave of Rebbe Nachman of Breslav, who spent the last few months of his short life (1772–1810) there. In Israel, his followers are often called "Na-nach-Nachman" because of a kind of mantra they intone. In the last few years, with the general resurgence of interest in Hassidism and other mystical and spiritual phenomena, tens of thousands of Jewish men from throughout the world – and not only Hassidim – fly to Uman to spend Rosh Hashanah in fervent mystical prayer at the gravesite. What I didn't know until my experience at the Kiev airport is that women also go to Uman, but at different times of the year, to ensure separation of the sexes.[1]

One of Rebbe Nachman's famous teachings is: it's a big mitzvah to always be happy. His followers often stand on street corners in Israeli cities, singing and dancing enthusiastically. For years, they used to be known as the "Dead Hassidim," because their leader, Rebbe Nachman, had died many decades (now centuries) earlier, but they weren't looking for a live replacement. I once heard someone say, "Better a dead rebbe with live Hassidim than a live rebbe with dead Hassidim." The Hassidim of Rebbe Nachman are very much alive.

It turned out that on our flight was a large group of Israeli women – mostly *Sephardiot* or *Mizrachiot* – who had just made the pilgrimage to Uman. They were a strong and cohesive group, but what I admired most about them was their spirit. They maintained their good humor and positive energy throughout this harrowing experience and encouraged us to sing and dance with them. I actually joined them and felt much better. After more than an hour in the forest, we were brought back to the terminal, to wait to board the flight. I looked for my book, but realized it had been confiscated when the police combed the airport, looking for the bomb. Of course, I could get a new copy at Yad Vashem, but it wouldn't be the same. I no longer have the beautiful dedication from my friend.

I arrived back in Israel in the middle of the night, but at least I got to spend that Shabbat at home. A few months later, the violence started in the Ukraine.

1. Perhaps we could say "so that it won't lead to mixed dancing."

Interfaith Week
in the United Kingdom

I N NOVEMBER OF 2009, Sir Sigmund Sternberg, the Patron of the ICCJ, and his wife, Lady Hazel, invited me to visit London to participate in "Interfaith Week in the UK" I have been to London quite a few times before and since, but this was certainly a very special trip. The program for the week involved a reception with the Archbishop of Canterbury at Lambeth Palace and a meeting in the House of Lords with a young man who, I believe, was at the time the first Muslim MP.

Eight or ten different religious groups were represented in the program. There were two other groups who were clamoring for recognition – the self-proclaimed Pagans and the Secular Humanists. At a lecture I gave during my visit, I was asked if I thought they or others could and should be included. My answer was that my criteria for inclusion would be: 1) If they are not actively preaching negation of other faith-communities or of faith in general, 2) If they provide for their members a sense of a supportive community that helps them get through the years of their lives, in which both joy and sorrow are shared together, then I would accept them into that framework. A colleague of mine from Poland suggests, as a third criterion, if they have succeeded in transmitting a sense of belonging or some type of heritage over at least three generations.

But definitely the highlight of my trip to London was something that came about serendipitously.

I have a friend named Colin, whom I met through his wife, Jean, a prominent Jewish educator. They were in Israel in 1989–1990 when she was a student on the Senior Educators Program at the Hebrew University Melton Centre for Jewish Education, where I taught. Colin's Ph.D. was in chemistry but he wrote several important books on the history of Zionism and became recognized as an expert in the field. I heard that during the short period I was to be in London in November, he was to be installed as the first Professor of Israel Studies at SOAS, the School for Oriental and African Studies at the University of London, which was establishing its first endowed Chair in Israel Studies. This seemed particularly noteworthy, as SOAS had developed a reputation for being virulently anti-Israel.

Thus it just so happened that I was in town for the installation and reception. I eagerly accepted the invitation. The hall was full, as Colin and key people from the SOAS administration marched in, wearing full academic regalia. They walked to the tune of the Beatles' "A Hard Day's Night" – in Yiddish. Colin later explained that he chose this background music to honor the memory of his parents, Eastern European Jewish immigrants to England. His father had been a tailor on the West End. And now the son was a professor at the University of London. And he gave an inaugural lecture on the history of antisemitism and anti-Zionism in the British Left.

That evening, SOAS hosted its first-ever kosher reception.

Lasting Effect? 1

I THINK THERE ARE TWO AREAS of my life in which I may have made a lasting contribution. Unfortunately, the achievement of peace in the Middle East isn't one of them. But changing the role and status of women in Jewish life definitely is.

I have no doubt that attending Barnard College in the late 1960s was essential to my developing a feminist consciousness, although I came ready for that from my family and home background. Before making *Aliyah*, I was one of the members of a small group called *Ezrat Nashim* in New York, the first Jewish religious feminist group in contemporary history. We chose the name because it refers to the women's section of an Orthodox synagogue and means, literally, "helping women." As Rabbi Yitz Greenberg pointed out to us, it is also the name of a mental hospital in Jerusalem, and he suggested that anyone who accepts the present role of women in Judaism belongs in such a place.

We were a group of ten to twelve women, mostly graduate students, who met for a few months of consciousness-raising and Talmud classes, with Judy Hauptman. The story of the group has been told in various articles, highlighting the "splash" we made at the Conservative Rabbinical Assembly conference at the Concord Hotel in March of 1972. We decided to "crash" this rabbinic conference, which was held before any of the American movements had yet begun to ordain women. (I believe that Regina Jonas had been ordained in Germany in 1935; she died several years later in Auschwitz.) All the other women at the conference were there as wives of rabbis. We set up a table in the lobby, organized some informal sessions, and did whatever else we could to try to put some of our concerns as women on the agenda. We did everything in a moderate and non-aggressive manner. Under normal circumstances, our appearance at the conference would hardly have been considered newsworthy. But there was a New York Times reporter present who chose to write about us, and we made the front page of the second section of the next day's paper. This threw us immediately into the national limelight. It necessitated us really "going public," setting up a speaker's bureau, and so on.

Half a year later, I was already living in Israel. At first, I felt very lonely in Israel as a religious feminist. I remember attending some general feminist gatherings that were often held over Shabbat, where I was usually the only observant woman present. Many of the women were very left-wing, and some even anti-Zionist. After the Yom Kippur War, someone suggested that we donate money to a fund for the welfare of the soldiers, and someone else said she'd rather burn the money than give it to that cause.

I was very fortunate to connect with Pnina Peli, who has been called "the mother of Jewish feminism." I had met her husband, Rabbi Pinchas Peli, in 1968, when he was a visiting professor in New York. I believe it isn't coincidental that he was a pioneer of inter-religious dialogue in Jerusalem, but in those days, I wasn't yet involved in that realm of his work. I became one of the regulars at their Shabbat table. During the mid-to-late 1970s, Pnina organized in their home women's prayer experiences, including the first women's celebrations of Simhat Torah in Jerusalem, during which we danced with the Torah and also read from it. In the late 1980s, she organized the first international conference on women and *Halakha*, out of which came the group known as Women of the Wall. Although I have had quite a few friends in that group, and I certainly support the right of women to pray at the Wall, I don't think it's always wise or judicious to exercise all of one's rights. There are other factors to be taken into consideration. I would apply that same reasoning, for example, to the right of Jews to live anywhere in the land of Israel or to pray on the Temple Mount.

We also started a women's religious feminist study group. The group met regularly and it was in that framework that I met Dr. Naomi Cohen. She was perhaps best-known for being the wife of the Chief Rabbi of Haifa, Rabbi She'ar Yashuv Cohen (who later also became very active in inter-religious dialogue circles). But Naomi was a scholar in her own right, taught Talmud in Haifa and saw herself as a feminist. In April 1978, I moved away from the neighborhood I had been living in since the summer of 1973, which was not far from the Pelis. I moved to the southeastern corner of West Jerusalem – first, Talpiot; then, Bak'a – where I have lived ever since. In 1980, we officially started Kehilat Yedidya, which in part reflected the influence of the Pelis, but I will discuss that separately.

Parallel to developments within women's Torah learning and ritual involvement, there were important advances in academic study of Jewish women. In general, the 1970s and 1980s were a time of great ferment for religious women in Israel. Several significant institutions of Torah learning for women or for women and men together were established – Pardes, Matan, Nishmat, etc. I have been privileged to both study and teach at some of them. In addition to the women I have already noted, mention must be made of the central role played by Professor Alice Shalvi. She took over the Pelech religious girls' high school, and transformed it into an experimental school and a bastion of feminism. Many leaders of the religious feminist movement in Israel are graduates of Pelech. I have always felt that education is the key to social change, especially in the area of women and Judaism.

An international conference on women's studies was held at the University of Haifa in 1981. I attended in my Army uniform and presented a paper on my *Bais Yaakov* research. That was the first of many such experiences, both in Israel and abroad. By 1985, I was teaching a course on Jewish women (the subtitle was "Traditions and Transitions") at the Hebrew University School for Overseas Students. I think it was the first university-level class in Jewish women's studies in Israel, although soon after, all of the major universities and many of the colleges began to offer programs in that area.

Every summer for over twenty years, the American Jewish Congress has held a dialogue session in Israel, involving Israeli and American Jews. I had never been invited to attend, but in 1984 I was invited, as the topic was: "Woman as Jew, Jew as Woman: An Urgent Inquiry." We joked that if the question was so urgent, why had they waited so long to deal with it? Out of that dialogue conference emerged what became known as the Israel Women's Network or *Sh'dulah*, Lobby, with Alice Shalvi at its head. Eight years later, Alice and I attended a weekend conference in a kosher hotel in Bournemouth in the south of England. It was a gathering of representatives from all the women's *Rosh Hodesh* groups in the UK. There is a tradition that women keep *Rosh Hodesh* in special ways, partly because women, like the moon, have their own monthly cycle (at least for a chunk of their lives). We were so impressed with these groups that when we came back to Jerusalem, we started a *Rosh Hodesh* group of our own in Jerusalem. It nourished us in many ways – socially, emotionally, intellectually, spiritually, maybe even ideologically – for thirteen years, but by 2005, we saw that the group meetings were no longer as satisfying as they had been, so we stopped.

Personally, the trip to Bournemouth was important for me in another way: I discovered, for the first time in my life, that I needed reading glasses; I was entering middle age.

By this time, Orthodox Jewish feminism was developing in North America in the form of JOFA, the Jewish Orthodox Feminist Alliance; one of its leaders was Blu Greenberg, whom I mentioned earlier. Partly as a result of an Israeli delegation that took part in a JOFA conference in New York in 1997 – I was among them – in 1998, the Israeli counterpart organization was founded, largely by (now Dr.) Hana Kehat. I attended the founding meeting. Naomi Cohen, whom I have mentioned, came out with a wonderful statement: "Feminism," she said, "is the radical idea that women are human beings." My friend Leah Shakdiel from Yerucham added, "And religious feminism is the even more radical idea that rabbis are human beings." We were off to a good start. The Israeli organization was called *Kolech*, "your voice," following our belief that women's voices should be heard.

It is not widely known that one of the people present at that gathering was Rav Aharon Lichtenstein, a prodigious Torah scholar and someone who later on would not support the more radical moves that *Kolech* made. Rav Lichtenstein was the son-in-law of the great Rav Yosef B. Soloveitchik. Beginning in Lithuania, the family for several generations had supported advanced Torah learning for women. At the founding of *Kolech*, he gave a talk in which he said that it's high time to stop questioning the sincerity of women who want to take on more active roles within Judaism. After all, he said, we don't question the motives of men who are seeking honors in the synagogue. That might not sound very "feminist" but I think it did advance our cause, since one of the common ways of delegitimizing Jewish feminists is to claim that we

Author's 40th birthday in 1987, with from left Tony Movshovitz and Aviva Zornberg

are not sincerely motivated religiously but are just pushing a political agenda.

I have my own story about the Soloveitchik family. In the early 1990s, when I was a doctoral student, a young master's student asked to make an appointment with me. Her name was Esty Rosenberg, which at the time meant nothing to me. She came to my office at the university and asked if I had done any research on Jewish women's education in Lithuania. My master's thesis, as I noted above, dealt with Poland. I offered her one piece of information I knew about Lithuania – that the Soloveitchik dynasty included some very learned women and encouraged women's Torah education. She never batted an eyelash.

I then told her about a certain book that would probably be helpful to her. Unfortunately, the only copy of that book in Jerusalem had been stolen from the National Library. I had managed to locate a copy of it in the Bar-Ilan library. Someone took it out for me and I photocopied the whole book, for my research. At this point, Esty said, "My mother teaches at Bar-Ilan. Perhaps she can help me."

Beginning to catch on, I asked, "What does she teach?" "Social work." I figured out that Esty's mother is Professor Tova Lichtenstein, wife of Rav Lichtenstein and daughter of Rav Soloveitchik. I thought that

Esty comported herself quite graciously, as befits the equivalent of Jewish nobility. *Noblesse oblige*. Probably the Soloveitchiks and their descendants – Esty went on to found the prestigious women's yeshiva, known as the Midrasha of Migdal Oz – have done more, both directly and indirectly, for the advancement of Jewish women's Torah learning than any other family in the history of Jewry.

My favorite story, summarizing the non-violent revolution that occurred within Jewish feminism, goes back to 1997. At the time, I was head of a teacher training program for Israeli high school teachers. One of my students invited me to her wedding, held on a religious kibbutz, not far from the one I had lived on thirty-one years earlier. At the ceremony, the rabbi, whom I respect and admire, gave the following sermonette: In the liturgy of the traditional Jewish wedding ceremony, we say, *"Kol Sasson v'kol Simcha, Kol Hatan v'kol Kallah."* This means, literally, "the voice of joy and the voice of gladness; the voice of the groom and the voice of the bride." Yet, he asked rhetorically, where in the traditional ceremony do we actually hear the voice of the bride? The bride is silent during the proceedings. This must be a prophecy, pointing to a better time in the future, when we will achieve real equality.

I thought to myself: Wow, this is good. I wish I would have given this talk. But when I discussed it afterwards with some other young women students, friends of the bride, they said: "Oh, no. This was just Orthodox apologetics. The couple went to the rabbi some time before the wedding, with a list of innovations for the ceremony, making it more egalitarian. He rejected all of their suggestions. He probably felt the need to make up for his refusal, so he gave this conciliatory speech."

I then said to the group," I have a little more perspective than you do. Ten years ago, the rabbi would not have felt a need to apologize; ten years from now, he'll institute the changes."

I don't know if I was right about this specific rabbi, as I have not since been to a wedding that he has done. But I have been to many other weddings, conducted by other Modern Orthodox rabbis in Israel, with changes much more far-reaching than what this couple asked to do. In fact, one of the most impressive areas in which the impact of feminism can be felt is all the Jewish life cycle ceremonies – those marking the birth of a baby girl, the Bat Mitzvah, the wedding, and the funeral and mourning rites. Having women as mere passive spectators has become, in most communities outside the *Haredi* (ultra-Orthodox) world, a thing

At a Jewish-Orthodox Christian consultation in Athens, 2015. Author is standing in the middle of the second row. Front row, seated from left: Rabbi David Rosen; Ms. Irit Ben-Abba, Israel's Ambassador to Greece; Metropolitan Emanuel.

of the past. Even at circumcision ceremonies of baby boys, women are becoming more involved. In 2009, at the circumcision of my nephew Nitzan's son, Matya Ami, I was given the great honor of holding the baby on a pillow on my lap. The Mohel – ritual "circumciser" – agreed for me to take this role, usually reserved for a grandfather. (The baby was given the second name of Ami after his late grandfather, who had been my brother-in-law and, in the meantime, my sister has been lucky enough to remarry.)

Although there have clearly been some important achievements, we still have a long way to go. And I'm not talking only about the injustices that still remain in the rabbinical courts which control Jewish marriage and divorce in this country. I'm also talking about the underrepresentation of women at meetings, conferences, and the like. I have been in many meetings on a variety of topics at which I am the only woman in the room. Being the only woman in a roomful of Jewish men is often more difficult than being the only Jew in a roomful of Christians.

THE OTHER CONTRIBUTION that has had a lasting effect is the creation of Kehillat Yedidya. I was one of its founders. Officially, we began in 1980; unofficially, the community was a product of a small group of young Jews in London who made *Aliyah* in the early 1970's. As graduate students, their London apartment had been a locus of Jewish religious activity in a more open or progressive fashion. By the mid-1970s, they and many of their friends had flocked to southeast Jerusalem which was just beginning to develop as an island of sanity in a difficult city. I moved to the area in 1978. What eventually became Yedidya was already meeting on special occasions such as Purim or Israel Independence Day, when it's permitted to travel, so they attracted people from other parts of the city, as well. For a few years, we also met during the High Holidays. We were the first mixed setting – mixed meaning men and women – in the Orthodox community in Jerusalem in which women danced with the Torah on *Simhat Torah*, in our own dance circles. In 1980, on that festival, we were so pleased with how things had been going that we began to discuss the possibility of establishing ourselves as a community and meeting on a regular basis, at least weekly. What followed was a year or so of intense ideological conversations and Saturday morning services. The following year, we added Friday nights; then, Shabbat afternoon; then, daily services. In 2003, we moved into our own building.

Not only was I one of the founding members, I was probably one of the three chief ideologues in the original group. One of them was the source for our name – Kehillat Yedidya. *Kehilla* means community in Hebrew and *Yedidya* is made up of two words, *yedid* – friend – and one of the names of the Lord. The idea was that we combine the social and the spiritual. The man who suggested our name stopped being Orthodox after a few years and left the community; another, Prof. Gerald Cromer, unfortunately died young of cancer. Another learned man joined after about five years and became a central figure. I remained involved and eventually initiated the formulation of our Principles (see Appendix C).

That first year, many people in the wider community didn't know quite what to make of us. Many people, in a display of ignorance, labeled us "Reform." We outgrew the initial venue in which we had been meeting and, for a time, met in a hall that was part of an Orthodox women's college. The administration there had a great deal of difficulty with our innovations in the area of women's participation, including when we had women giving sermons ("*divrei Torah*"). I have a good friend who was also one of the initial members. He may have been a feminist all along – it was probably his mother's influence – but certainly with the birth of his two daughters, he became a strong advocate for women's involvement. I remember going with him to a meeting with the two Chief Rabbis of our neighborhood to discuss our policy on *divrei Torah*. In most places in the world where there is a Chief Rabbinate, there is one Chief Rabbi. In Israel, in most places, there are two – one *Ashkenazi* and one *Sephardi*. I was in the Army at the time and I wore my uniform to the meeting.

I told the rabbis that all day long, I teach Judaism to officers and officers-in-training and you're telling me I can't do it in my own community. One of the rabbis offered a suggestion, "I don't see why you have to give the *d'var Torah* yourself. Why don't you just write it out and have your husband read it?" It seemed futile to try to explain.

We reached a compromise with the administrators. They agreed to allow women to speak once the official service was over. So we decided that we would simply move the timing of the sermon, from right before the Torah reading, to the end of the service. This would be the case for both women and men. Then, they demanded that when a woman gets up to speak, we have to remove the Torah from the room. We decided that we couldn't live with that ruling and looked for another place to meet, landing in the neighborhood community center entrance hall. After a while, we moved again, and then again, finally ending up in the basement of a local religious elementary school, where we stayed for eighteen years. Eventually we realized that we needed our own building. I served as Co-Chair of the Fundraising Committee. It was a long haul, but the building began to be constructed in 2000 and, despite the Second Intifada which slowed things down, we moved in during August of 2003.

Yedidya has never hired a rabbi, although we've had many rabbis, both male and female, as members of the community. There are other congregations, especially in Israel, that don't have a rabbi. In the Diaspora, in most places, you need a rabbi who serves as the most knowledgeable Jew in the community. He (or she) may be the only person qualified to lead services, read from the Torah, give a sermon, and so on. We thankfully have many people who can do some or all of the above. In more traditional frameworks, you may also need a rabbi in order to make Halakhic decisions in the area of practice. When a rabbi makes such a decision, he is generally balancing the textual sources he has studied for years, his perception of what's appropriate for the particular setting in question, and his own views. We consulted with rabbis who could give us a sense of the parameters of the *Halakha*. But we felt that in terms of perceiving what's appropriate, who would know that better than the community itself?

Once, sometime in the 1990s, a question arose as to whether women could be given the honor of opening and closing the Holy Ark during the High Holiday services. There were two prominent Orthodox rabbis in our congregation at the time, so we consulted with them on this issue. One said yes; the other said no. To me, this was a clear example of their general views and attitudes on women's issues. Once we moved into our own building in 2003, we instituted the innovation of women, on many occasions, opening and closing the Ark.

Initially, our decisions about our own practices and customs as a community were made in the almost interminable group discussions we held together. After a while, as the community structures began to become more formalized in general, we set up a committee to deal with matters of *Halakha* and *Minhag* (Jewish laws and customs). I served as chairperson of that committee for about fifteen to twenty years. Thankfully, in December of 2014, I finally stepped down.

The model our committee represents is unusual. I am not referring only to the concept of *Da'at Torah* in the *Haredi* world, in which rabbis know best about everything, including for whom to vote in national elections. I am referring as well to the concepts of rabbinic authority prevalent within the modern Orthodox community today – and I have heard even Conservative and Reform rabbis speaking in the name of rabbinic authority, although for the Reform, this has a distinctly non-Halakhic character. The Orthodox rabbi, by virtue of his immersion in traditional Torah texts, is considered to possess authority not only in matters of *Halakha*, but also of meta-*Halakha* and even of public policy.

In 1980, Yedidya made a principled decision not to seek a rabbi who would serve as the authority figure for the community. Our model for this was the Religious Kibbutz movement prior to the 1970s. In those early kibbutzim, rabbis were consulted as Halakhic resources and guides, but decisions were taken by the community as a unit, in recognition of the fact that many of the issues involved extra-Halakhic considerations of a more ideological nature (e.g., army service for women, reliance on work by non-Jews on Shabbat, etc.)

In Yedidya, rabbis have been consulted in order to sketch out the possible Halakhic parameters of a particular issue. There are quite a few ordained rabbis, both male and female, who are members of the community. But when there were public policy considerations involved, it was felt that the rabbi's voice should not be more or less authoritative or dominant than that of any other adult member of the congregation (male or female). In a democratic society, in which whole Torah libraries are available to us on the computer, and in a community such as Yedidya, in which the average member has a graduate academic degree, the role of the rabbi as ultimate authority in questions of policy, as distinguished from *Halakha*, can begin to be challenged.

In an article comparing university research in Talmud with traditional Yeshiva learning, Professor Menachem Kahana encouraged a gradual process of "democratization and the transfer of some of the authority for Halakhic decision-making from the rabbi as advisor and guide to the individual and the community."[1]

One of the important events in the history of Yedidya involved a break-away group that established the first "partnership *Minyan*" in Israel known as *Shira Hadasha*, during the fall-winter of 2000–2001. They took all the initial innovations we had made and carried them

---

1. In a book called *B'chavlei Massoret u'Temura*, Rehovot: Kivunim, 1990, p.133 (my translation).

further in the direction of egalitarianism. At first, I must admit that I resented them for two reasons: (1) It seemed to me that they hadn't tried, at least not officially, to introduce more innovations at Yedidya. They had, for example, never approached our committee – perhaps they decided that Yedidya couldn't abide the changes and so they had to start a new synagogue. (2) They invested a great deal of effort – and perhaps money – in public relations and made quite a splash. Soon after they started, a full-page article about them appeared in the *HaAretz* newspaper. We had been lonely and unrecognized for twenty years before they came upon the scene and the news of their existence spread quickly throughout the Jewish world.

I had a funny personal experience in this regard. In the autumn of 2003, I was on a speaking tour in the U.K. I was scheduled to teach at a *Bet Midrash* sponsored by *B'nei Akiva* in London. The most impressive thing for me on that evening was that in this *Bet Midrash*, there were some eighty young men and women sitting and learning Jewish texts; some of them appeared to have Down's syndrome. They were fully integrated into the learning groups; this brought tears to my eyes.

When it came time for a young man to introduce me to the audience, he asked, "On your CV, it says you were one of the founders of Yedidya – is that like *Shira Hadasha?*"

I would add, however, that I have long since gotten over my resentment. Quite the contrary – I think that Yedidya can be proud; imitation is considered to be the sincerest form of flattery. The positive feeling seems to be mutual now. In 2014, *Shira Hadasha* hosted a conference of twenty or so partnership *Minyanim* both here and abroad; they invited me to chair one of the central panels. We received due credit publicly for our work as pioneers.

In 2003, as we were about to move into our own building, I wrote the following to our members about the above:

"Recently someone told me that she heard our shul characterized as a bunch of '*hafifnikim.*' That's Hebrew slang for superficially religious people who try to get by with the minimum. I don't think that's a fair characterization at all. It's not that I'm uncritical of Yedidya. As anyone who has ever attended a Va'ad meeting with me (or discussed shul business with me in any forum) can ascertain, I tend to be quite critical – it's an extended kind of self-criticism. But we are most assuredly not *hafifnikim.* That term typically describes people who were brought up religious and who have remained so sociologically, but without much depth. I think most of us are the opposite. Many (if not most) of us came either from non-religious homes, or from homes less religious than we are or, at least, less Zionist. The fact that there are so many *olim* in our community means something, as does the range of professions (most of us tend to be in the intellectual, non-lucrative professions). We want the synagogue to be a place for meaningful intellectual, emotional, spiritual and social-cultural expression, not just a place we drop in on because we were brought up that way and can't really conceive of anything else.

If I had to use one phrase to describe the nature and vision of the founders of the community, as well as the majority of "newer" people who have remained involved over the years, it would be "religious humanists." That describes a pretty broad range of role models, which may include Shimshon Raphael Hirsch, Shmuel David Luzzatto, Henrietta Szold, Abraham J. Heschel, Martin Buber, David Hartman, but also, I hope, Ben Azzai, Rabbi Yehoshua ben Levi, the Rambam and many others (since we're approaching Shavuot, maybe I should add: Naomi?).

The basic text for religious humanists is Genesis 1:27, about the creation of human beings, all human beings, male and female, in the image of God. I don't have to add "Jew and non-Jew" because it's quite clear that there were no Jews at the time, and that the intention is *all* human beings. Religious humanists, I believe, must take very seriously anything which enhances the dignity of human beings, like democracy and feminism. They must reject anything which denigrates the human being, like racism and sexism. On that basis, I would maintain, the founders of Yedidya built a community in which women could be first-class citizens, non-Jews could be welcome guests, issues of democracy and human rights could be taken seriously and the pursuit of peace could be recognized as a religious imperative. People who give *d'rashot* could quote non-Jewish sources (or non-Orthodox Jewish sources) unapologetically. *Halakha* and ethics could be seen as not mutually exclusive categories. And, may I add: the religiosity of the community would be measured not by the length of our sleeves but by the way we treat people with disabilities, the way we help people in need, our commitments to prayer, study and *Tzedakah*, the amount we gossip (actually, quite minimally, I'm happy to say), the extent to which we open our homes to guests (quite maximally). Anyway, I'm certainly not suggesting that there's only one way for religious humanists to vote or to resolve political questions or to decide on separate women's Torah readings vs. *Shira Hadasha*-style davening. I actually believe that there exists such a thing as right-wing humanists – one of my sociological mentors, Peter Berger, fits into this category. I also recognize that equality doesn't necessarily imply sameness. But I can't conceive of a religious humanist ignoring human rights issues or being totally indifferent to questions of women's equality."

There is a general consensus that the move was beneficial and that now we have a beautiful sanctuary and lots of space for all kinds of activities. It also has meant that we are much less informal in the way we run things – I've had some problems with that. But a bigger problem for me has been that over the years, the composition of the community has changed. I think it's wonderful that we have attracted younger people – post-Baby Boomers – including Israeli families (initially, most of the native Israelis were spouses of immigrants). But, for a long time, we simply opened our doors to anyone who wanted to join, sometimes not even making them aware of the special nature of the synagogue. Some people are attracted by the fact that you can get by without knowing Hebrew, it's convenient for them, we have very good children's activities, we have a weekly Kiddush, and many other things that don't have much to do with ideology. I think that the change reflects some broader phenomena as well – the world in general and Israel in particular, are less ideological. These days, the new immigrants coming from the West tend to be far more right-wing than those who came in the 60s and 70s. Some changes in the role of women in the synagogue are now more accepted in mainstream Orthodoxy, at least in certain places, and therefore we are no longer perceived by some as being so innovative.

My personal reaction to these changes has made me more empathetic towards the old-timers of the Kibbutz movement. Although they never represented more than a small percentage of our population, kibbutzim used to be a symbol of Israel and Zionism, a cultural elite in our society, a source of political and military leadership, and what Martin Buber called "an experiment that didn't fail."

During the 1980s, a process of privatization changed the Kibbutz movement dramatically. One of the results is that in the Knesset that was elected in 2013, there were no kibbutz members at all. I feel a sense of identification with the founders of many of the kibbutzim. They have become conservative or even reactionary in their commitment to socialism and collectivism. But if the majority of the kibbutz's members want to privatize, and decisions are reached democratically, what can you do? I sometimes feel that way about what is happening at Yedidya. If the majority wants to change the character of the community, is there anything we can do democratically to prevent that from happening?

In 2005, Yedidya undertook a lengthy and thorough process of introspection and deliberation to see if we wanted to move in the direction of *Shira Hadasha*. The specific question was on having women and men participate in mixed Torah readings. Our practice up until then had been (and still is) to hold a separate women's Torah reading approximately once a month, often for special occasions such as a Bat Mitzvah. We studied the issue, held discussions and finally "voted" through an e-mail questionnaire. We asked our members to indicate not only what their personal preference would be but also how they would respond if some other decision were to be taken.

Some people who objected vigorously to mixed readings threatened to leave if we went in that direction. It became clear that the overwhelming majority of Yedidya members were so committed to the value of keeping the community together, that this took preference over their desire for change. We left the status quo, but without a clear commitment for the future. For eight years, we continued, growing and developing the basement of our building into an additional floor for activities. The volume of social and cultural activities, as well as charitable projects, increased. I personally think that the quality of our communal prayers improved, as we began to have more qualified and experienced leaders. The two major foci of debate centered around politics and homosexuality. The homosexual question became the theme of a series that we sponsored, one of the first Orthodox communities to deal with the issue in a sensitive and sympathetic manner.

Politically, the volatility of the issues in Israel affected us deeply. We held many conversations, both face-to-face and electronically, on the settlements, the peace process, the fighting in Gaza, etc. Eventually, we started a group of about a dozen members (I was one of them), representing right, left and center positions on Israeli politics, who met regularly to try to listen to and understand each other.

I am stressing all of this because in 2013, when our committee raised the suggestion for women to lead the *Kabbalat* Shabbat service at Yedidya, some of the opponents to the change made the following case,

"I joined a congregation that did A, B and C, but not D." Never mind that A and B were already more radical *halakhically* than the newly proposed change would be. The opponents admitted quite early on that it wasn't a Halakhic problem for them so much as an emotional one. The opponents weren't necessarily more observant or more learned than the supporters (actually, most of the learned members of the community supported the change). They are just more conservative and less open to change. Sometimes, this goes together with more conservative politics, but that isn't always the case.

During the year of 2013–2014, we had an even lengthier process of deliberation than the last time. We offered several panels, discussion groups and an Internet poll. The result was that for the time being, we are running two parallel services, about once a month – one in which *Kabbalat* Shabbat is led by a woman and one in which it's led by a man. Men and women have the choice of which to attend, with almost two-thirds going to the women's-led service.

The process took a huge toll on me. I felt that many of the opponents of the change were attacking me personally, impugning both my religious sincerity and my integrity as a person. It was the most difficult moment I had ever experienced at Yedidya. Although we had conducted what seemed like an interminable process of deliberation, one veteran member quit the community because he felt we hadn't discussed the issue enough. But rather than dwell on this, I would like to consider the ways in which I believe we have had a lasting effect on Israeli society or even more broadly:

(1) I have no doubt that we have influenced Modern Orthodoxy across the globe with regard to the status of women in current Halakhic practice. In this respect we have at the very least earned our place in Jewish history, if not also in the World-to-Come, both directly and indirectly, through *Shira Hadasha* and the other partnership *Minyanim*.

(2) We were one of the first synagogues in Jerusalem to stress the creation of a real community and not just a place for prayer. This undoubtedly reflects the fact that so many of us are immigrants who needed a replacement for our extended families. Over the years, we have endured together catastrophic illnesses that befell members and their children, fatal accidents, wars and intifadas. New generations of children and then grandchildren have emerged.

(3) Similarly, we blazed a trail with respect to pluralism within

Judaism. While still a problematic and sometimes painful issue, at the very least on the local level, our community serves as an example of an Orthodox community which co-operates fruitfully with Jews of different persuasions. In 1986, the *Simhat Torah* celebrations at a neighboring Reform congregation were disrupted by the local Orthodox rabbi, whose followers grabbed a *Sefer Torah* out of the hands of a woman. Several months later, we invited that community to join us for a joint *Tu B'Shevat* Seder. It earned us a piece in the Jerusalem Post, although of course that wasn't our motivation.

(4) Apropos pluralism, there is no question that we are particularly active in the field of interfaith activity, and in particular, hosting non-Jewish groups. In this we have served as an inspiration to some of our neighbors in other congregations. I believe we can count hundreds and even thousands of people who now have, through a first-hand experience, a different image of Judaism and Israel. There are at least five members of Yedidya who work full-time in inter-religious and inter-cultural dialogue, and many more who do so occasionally. I'm sure we are the only shul – and maybe the only congregation of any kind – in the world to have had in its membership two past presidents of the ICCJ – Rabbi David Rosen and me.

(5) Our *Beit Knesset* – synagogue – was the first in Jerusalem and perhaps in the whole country which was totally accessible to people with physical disabilities. This building has been recognized by many as exemplar in this respect, and we were also the first Orthodox community in the world to install an FM hearing loop which allows the hearing-impaired to participate fully. Many settings have such a loop, but we were the first to obtain a system that is authorized for Shabbat use by an institute for technology and *Halakha*.

(6) There are few Orthodox synagogues that organize art exhibitions. In some of the more traditional sectors of the Orthodox community, art itself is quite suspect from a religious point-of-view. Yedidya does hold periodic exhibits, partly because we have quite a few artists, writers and musicians within the community itself. Our exhibitions attract people who don't normally set foot inside a *Beit Knesset*. A few years ago, when we held an exhibition of calligraphy which included Arabic and Chinese, I felt extremely proud to be a member of the community.

(7) I will mention another aspect, but it's controversial: this is the social-political one. From what I've already mentioned – about the status

Author with Linda Gradstein, at Linda's wedding to
Cliff Churgin, 1991, photo by Debbi Cooper

of women, different movements in Judaism, interfaith relationships, consideration for those with handicaps, and also perhaps aesthetic values, we can pinpoint a single common denominator – respect for all human beings *as a religious value*, all people as God's creatures. But it is not always clear what this means in political terms. There is a certain tension between the liberal politics of many of our members, in particular of the founding members, and that of the overall pluralism of the community. Most Orthodox communities in Israel distribute on Shabbat many leaflets that give interpretations of the weekly Torah portion. Usually, these are published by organizations and institutions that offer only right-wing and sometimes extremist perspectives. Personally I am happy that we distribute the left-leaning "Shabbat Shalom" as our preferred *daf parshat hashavua* and that the editor and many of the writers are Yedidya members.

Not a little has been accomplished. Particularly if one takes into account the fact that we employ almost no staff, and that almost all that has been done has been carried out by volunteers, we really do have something to be proud of.

I will conclude with some comments made by a sympathetic outsider. Dr. Elana Sztokman is an important scholar of gender studies and Jewish education. Her first book was a re-working of her doctorate and was called, *The Men's Section: Orthodox Jewish Men in an Egalitarian World* (University Press of New England, the Hadassah Brandeis Institute, 2011). In the book, there is an unflattering portrayal of how some men behave in some synagogues during the Torah reading. Eager to make sure that the Torah reader makes no mistakes in the reading, they may "bark" their corrections. Elana writes that for some, this has turned into a kind of "sport." I told her that I hadn't experienced that at Yedidya. This is how she responded, in February of 2013:

". . . I think the fact that your shul doesn't bark is a testament to your culture. From the few times I've been to Yedidya my impression was that it really is a whole different culture than Orthodoxy. I think Yedidya has been challenging the patriarchal culture in much more subtle ways than simply allowing women to lead. I think that Yedidya embraces that gentleness, the one that feels antithetical to Orthodoxy in many of these circles. That's a lot of what I was trying to say. You know, that there is an entire persona of masculinity that dominates Orthodox life, that has to do with this aggressive, emotionless, unquestioning obedience rather than with a deeper vision of spirituality. So the gentleness with which Yedidya embraces *layners* (Torah readers – D.W.), I think is a very subtle but very significant expression of the fact that Yedidya has recognized this dynamic and challenged it for a very long time."

Retirement in Jerusalem

I OFTEN JOKE THAT RETIRED means "re-tired"; tired again. As many retirees do, I wonder how I ever found time to work. To some people, the fact that I'm retired is a source of great surprise, because I'm still quite active. As I point out to them, retired doesn't mean dead.

I took retirement the first moment I could, at 61 years, 8 months. For the first six years or so of my retirement, I served as President of the ICCJ. In that role, I traveled a lot. In 2009, the Inter-religious Coordinating Council in Israel sent a three-person delegation on a speaking tour to Australia. Although one of our goals was fund-raising, and we totally failed at that, the talks we gave were largely successful. We were a Muslim Israeli man from Abu Ghosh, who later went on to become its mayor, a Christian Palestinian woman from East Jerusalem, and me.

We spoke several times a day over the course of a couple of weeks, appearing on the radio in four languages – English, Hebrew, Arabic and Yiddish. Our lectures were given in schools, universities, churches, synagogues, inter-religious dialogue groups and other settings. Issa, the Muslim, would sometimes begin by telling the audience: "In front of you are two Israelis and two Palestinians. But, you might say, there are only three people on stage. That's not because my math is wrong, but because I am both Israeli and Palestinian." This certainly broke down some stereotypes, as did exposure to the concept and reality of Palestinian *Christian* communities.

Several months later, I ran a seminar in Israel for the ICCJ called "From Two Narratives to Building a Culture of Peace." We had participants from six different countries. One of the ways of keeping our costs down was by accommodating the group half of the time in people's homes – two nights in Abu Ghosh and two nights in Jerusalem. In Jerusalem, they stayed with friends of mine, mainly from Yedidya. In Abu Ghosh, my friend Issa arranged the home hospitality.

One of the things I do a lot of now is study, everything from Talmud to languages to European cinema. Jewish texts are often read together with a *hevruta*, a study partner. *Hevruta* is an Aramaic word that means a kind of close friend. I have three close friends with whom – one-on-one – over the years I have studied various classical Jewish texts and even books of the New Testament. One of them is my friend Marcie. Although we had been learning together for a long time, it turned out that one of the things we had never discussed was who cuts our hair. We learned later that we have the same hairdresser. He's a religious guy from Manchester – probably a *Ba'al Teshuva* – with a black *kippa*. One day I happened to run into Marcie in the beauty parlor. The three of us – she, the hairdresser and I – discussed some Torah he had been learning that week. That seemed to me to be a typically Jerusalem story.

I have two other typical stories: One year, during the very busy days before Pesach, I needed to go into one of the ultra-Orthodox neighborhoods to buy ground carp in order to make gefilte fish. It's on the other side of town, and I didn't want the fish to go bad, so I hopped into a taxi to take me home. Next to the driver was an ultra-Orthodox Jew with a black skullcap and a long white beard; they let me sit in the back. The two of them were having a lively conversation in Hebrew, and I couldn't help but hear it. Frequently, the driver would say things like, "thank God," or "with the help of God." After a while, the other passenger remarked that the driver seemed to be a deeply religious person and asked, "So, why aren't you wearing a *kippa*?" The driver answered, "Because I'm not Jewish."

My guess is that he was probably a Muslim.

Years later, on a Friday morning, I went to the supermarket that is diagonally across from my home. Because Friday is the busiest day of the week, the store places extra workers at the counter to help pack your grocery bags. One particular Friday, I noticed that the worker wasn't packing my bottles of wine. I'm embarrassed to say that my first reaction was, "Some religious Jews are worried that non-Jews will handle their wine bottles. Some silly person must have told him not to touch the bottles."

Then, immediately, I realized that as a devout Muslim, he wouldn't handle bottles of wine or alcohol. I would never characterize the beliefs of a different religion as silly – then, why my own? Anyway, while I was going through this entire thought process, I forgot to pay and was preparing to leave the store, when the owner – a Jew – stopped me. I said, "Yes, of course, 'Thou shalt not steal.'" And he added, "That's in this week's Torah portion."

For much of 2011–2012, we in Israel were caught up in a fierce debate about Iran. Many people I know, including some who are left-wing on the issues of the settlements and the West Bank, were deathly afraid of a nuclear attack by the Iranians. Several of our leading politicians and most prominently our Prime Minister, built themselves up around this fear, portraying a nuclear Iran as the greatest existential threat to our survival.

I had a different take on the issue. I grew up in the 1950s and 1960s in America, under the shadow of the Bomb. We had air raid drills in elementary school. I remember the questions, "Would you rather be Red or dead?" and "Which people would you let into your bomb shelter?" In October of 1962, during the height of the Cuban missile crisis, I remember saying good-bye to my 10th grade classmates on Friday and not knowing if we would see each other again on Monday. But since the bombings of Hiroshima and Nagasaki in 1945 – by the United States, it should be noted – nuclear weapons have not been used in any world conflict.

What scared the wits out of me was the possibility that Israel would launch a pre-emptive attack on Iran. When Ehud Barak estimated that we could withstand a retaliatory attack, in which "only" tens of thousands of our population would be killed in the first few minutes, I shuddered at the thought.

August of 2012 started out as a regular month in my life. When I say "regular," I mean, for example, that one evening, I attended the wedding of the daughter of some friends. The event was held at a lovely place on the outskirts of Jerusalem. I had a taxi pick me up at the wedding to take me to the airport for a 1:20 flight to Brussels, arrived early in the morning and took a train to Leuven, in time for a breakfast meeting.

After two days of inter-religious meetings in Leuven, I came back for Shabbat at home.

But then, on August 19th, while I was doing a routine self-examination, I felt a small lump in my left breast. For the next few months, I didn't think at all about Iran.

I had a lumpectomy and twenty-one radiation treatments. I did not need chemotherapy. I now take Tamoxifen and have regular visits to an oncologist. However, the experience with cancer seems to have had very little influence on my life and my views. One thing did change, but it had less to do with the cancer than with a twenty-seven-week cold.

Less than a month after receiving the results of the biopsy, I caught a bad cold. I was convinced that this had something to do with my overall immune system, although the oncologist disagreed. I went to a series of specialists, but nothing helped. During this time, a friend from London came for a visit. She is very much into health foods, alternative treatments, and that sort of thing. She suggested that I might try something alternative. I snapped back at her, "They only work if you believe in them, and I don't."

It was now March, about ten days before Pesach (Passover), and not only did I have acute allergic rhinitis, but I lost my voice. Typically, I make the Seder in my home and lead it for my family. How could I do that without being able to talk and to sing? So, I went to my GP and asked him if he could possibly recommend someone who has an MD, but also does alternative stuff. I suppose you could say I'd become desperate.

He gave me the name of someone who practices both conventional Western and Chinese medicine. After my first acupuncture session, I regained my voice. I continued going to him for several months, for a combination of acupuncture and Chinese herbs. It worked. He admitted that he doesn't know how or why, but it does. I later apologized to my friend and went back to worrying about Iran.

As a result of my illness, I have not changed my diet or my lifestyle, but I have become far less cynical about non-conventional therapies. Something I believed before has been re-enforced: the term "cancer" should never be used to refer to human beings. Cancer is a complex of diseases and disorders that affect the cells of our bodies and should not become a metaphor for other things we don't like. Similarly, I really dislike the over-use of the term "DNA." It's become quite popular, even among liberals, in Israel to say things like, "This is in our cultural DNA," or "It's part of our DNA as Jews." I find that borders on racism. Values and culture are not transmitted through genetic material.

For many years, almost every weekday at 2 p.m., the radio has broadcast a program called, in Hebrew, "Magic Moments." It is an hour of "oldies, but goodies." The implication of that phrase, of course, is that if something is old, it can't really be good, making these songs exceptional. Obviously, I believe that "good "and "old" can go together, and I love the program.

I also tend to watch more television than any of my friends, whether they are still working or are already retired. I watch *Arutz HaKnesset*, the Knesset channel, almost daily. It isn't just a channel that televises Knesset sessions and committees, although it does that, too. And they're sometimes rather interesting.

But, additionally, they have excellent analyses, interviews, discussion programs, documentaries, etc. There is a lot of room on the channel for voices of the opposition.

I have also gained some respect for the Knesset and how it works. There is a fair amount of bi- or multi-partisanship. Although on issues of the territories, the right and left wings are diametrically opposed, and secularists and Orthodox differ on religion and state, on most other questions, there's a lot of agreement: the environment, for example, women's and children's rights, and many other domestic issues.

One of the members of the 19th Knesset (2013–2015), Dr. Ruth Calderon, is a friend of mine from my Army days. In 2014, she established a group that met weekly in the Knesset library for the study of Jewish texts. Within the group were men and women, religious and secular. At her invitation, I joined this group. Unfortunately, after I had been there only twice – for two excellent study sessions – the Prime Minister called for new elections and the Knesset disbanded. The study sessions ended. Ruth wasn't re-elected.

In 2014, I stepped down after two terms of the ICCJ Presidency. I wrote the following in my final President's report:

> "I would like to share with you a brief word of Torah. It is based on an interesting turn-of-phrase in the 4th chapter of Leviticus. The general topic is sin-offerings. In all but one of the cases mentioned – e.g., the anointed priest, the whole congregation, any one of the common people

Opening the ICCJ conference in Rome, 2015. From left: Conference Co-Chair Marco Morcelli; Cardinal Giuseppe Betori, the Archbishop of Florence; author; Rabbi Abraham Skorka, and Conference Co-Chair and ICCJ President, Professor Philip Cunningham. Photo courtesy of ICCJ.

Author receiving honorary doctorate from the Hebrew Union College in Jerusalem, 2014. From left: with author (holding scroll,) international leadership of HUC Rabbis Michael Marmur, Aaron Panken, Na'ama Kelman (partially obscured) and Dalia Marx. Photo by Yitzhak Harrari.

At the annual ICCJ conference in Buenos Aires, 2014, with the Sternberg Interfaith Gold Medallion, photo courtesy of ICCJ

– the text says "*if* they sin . . ." In other words, it's a *possibility* that they may sin. But with regard to the *Nasi*, the President, it says, "*when* he (I would add: or she) sins and makes a mistake . . ." As some of our commentators have pointed out, it is a *certainty* that the President will make mistakes. So, I would like to apologize to all those whom I've hurt or offended in this role. These were unintentional, honest mistakes."

The organization decided to honor me with the Sternberg Interfaith Gold Medallion, "Peace through Dialogue." I wish that this medallion could celebrate some real achievements rather than just efforts to achieve peace. Several months later, I received an honorary doctorate from the Hebrew Union College in Jerusalem. Some people have taken to calling me "Dr.Dr." or "Double Doctor" or even "Dr. Squared." Especially since HUC is a Reform institution and I am but a sympathetic outsider, I consider this a great honor (see Appendix D).

I made *Aliyah* to a largely secular, left-leaning country where the kibbutz movement was disproportionately influential. I now live in a right-wing, religious and traditional society, where there are almost no traces left of socialism and where racism is on the rise. But, as I have tried to show, in some ways, it's better now. We have much more religious pluralism, feminist values that are anchored in progressive legislation, something that's been called a Jewish cultural renaissance and more room for all kinds of people who previously were confined to the periphery.

I omitted altogether the fact that on every material level, things have improved. When I first came, we had to bring with us cans of tuna fish, rolls of soft toilet paper, aluminum foil, and other things that weren't available, even for lots of money. Over the years, just about everything became available, albeit expensive, except for fresh Brussels sprouts, so I buy them frozen. In the 1960s, dining out wasn't yet a popular thing in Jerusalem; in fact, I remember going out on a Saturday night and buying the trendy snack, which at the time was oily potato pancakes! Now, we have every kind of restaurant, and some of them are even good. Or, very good. In the 1980s, for a time, we had the world's only Kosher Indonesian restaurant, but I was one of only a very few people who patronized it, so, after a short while, they closed. But if you want Kosher Italian, Chinese, Japanese, Indian, Thai, etc., we've got it. And don't you just have to love a country where the supermodel is named Esty Ginzburg?

Our city also has something that may be unique in the developed world. I like cities, but I also like quiet. The quiet of Yom Kippur and, to a slightly lesser degree, Friday afternoon and Shabbat morning, in Jerusalem is, I believe, unparalleled in the world's other major capitals.

I live in a complex of ten buildings. Each building has at least twelve apartments, and some have twenty to thirty. We're talking about a population of hundreds or more, probably more. One Friday afternoon in September of 2014, I was walking about in our complex around the time of Sabbath candle-lighting. It was completely silent. We have a great deal of vegetation in the center of the complex. The setting sun shone on the plants in a magical way. I thought, "How lucky we are; I wish everyone in the world could experience such quiet beauty." People do, for example, on the savannah in Africa, but not usually in a Western-style world capital rapidly approaching its first million inhabitants.

Many of the cities I like most in the world have a combination of mountains and a beach – for example, Sydney, Capetown, Vancouver, San Francisco, Haifa. Jerusalem is exceptional in this respect – lots of hills, with little water to speak of, and certainly no beach. It does have fascinating and beautiful architecture from many different periods of history. It also has great natural beauty, I think. One of the loveliest things I have ever seen was a Jerusalem courtyard after a big winter storm, where a palm tree's branches sagged under the weight of the snow.

In our liturgy the city most frequently mentioned is, of course, Jerusalem. On our festivals, we recite Psalms of praise called *Hallel*, including the following: "How can I answer the Lord for all His benefits towards me? . . . I will pay my vows unto the Lord in the presence of all His people; in the courts of the Lord's house, *in the midst of thee, O Jerusalem . . .*" I have never become jaded with regard to praying about the city in which I live.

One of the facts that long-term Jerusalem residents know, but others might not be aware of, is that in about 90% of the cases, the neighborhoods and street names are organized around specific themes. I live in Bak'a, a biblically-themed neighborhood, on the corner of Rebecca Street and Bethlehem Road. There are other neighborhoods organized around the Mishna, medieval rabbis, the 1948 war, pro-Zionist Gentiles, flowers, etc. If you know a little about Jewish history and someone tells you their street name, you can usually, with only a few exceptions, guess what neighborhood they live in. Thus, even walking around the streets turns into an educational experience.

I have mentioned several of the factors that make my life in Jerusalem so special – our community, my friends and study partners, hosting people from all over the world for Shabbat and festivals, my teaching and so on. But it's also the city itself, one of the world's most fascinating and varied. There's always something new or different, and some of the newest things are among the most ancient. It's a multicultural, multiethnic, multilingual and, of course, multi-religious city. I celebrate its diversity; I wish everyone else would at least tolerate it.

A Hopeful Pessimist

FOR A WHILE, I used to collect amusing statements about optimists and pessimists, thinking that I belonged to the former group. For example, former Israeli president Shimon Peres said, "Optimists and pessimists die the same death; they just live totally different lives." There's also a story I used to tell about two friends. The first asked the second, "Are you an optimist or a pessimist?" The second replied, "I'm an optimist." The first asked, "Then, why do you look so upset?" To which the second answered, "You think it's so easy to be an optimist?" Additionally, I used to quote the Hebrew joke, "I'm short, so I see the half of the cup that's full."

But I've realized recently that I'm really a pessimist, albeit a hopeful one. Mike Rosenak used to say that Jews are pessimists in the short run and optimists, in the long run. Perhaps that's what I am.

What has made me feel pessimistic recently is the realization that I probably won't live long enough to see peace in this region. That's a very sobering thought. I'm not referring only to the horrific situation in the Middle East in general. It has become a cliché to say that the Arab Spring has turned into a dark and depressing winter. I mourn for the hijacking of Islam by violent, repressive forces, and the plight of Christians and other minority groups in our region. I'm referring in particular to the Israeli-Palestinian conflict. I think that the settlements in the territories have been a major strategic mistake on the part of the State of Israel. Many of the people who went to live in them are fine, decent but, I think, misguided. I'm not angry with most of them; I'm angry at the political leadership of this country (Labor as well as Likud) for what has happened. I'm angry at the political leaders for having destroyed my chance to see peace.

Of course, it's not only Israel's fault. Neither is it only the fault of the Palestinians, nor the Arabs, nor the Muslims. I do think we have all missed some important opportunities. Terror and violence directed at any innocent population are despicable.

2002 was probably the worst year we experienced here. It was the lowest point of the Second Intifada. Pesach, which I usually enjoy, was awful – perhaps symbolically, it rained for the full week, but the worst moment was the Seder night, when a homicide bomber – I think that's a more apt phrase than "suicide bomber" – blew himself up in the lobby of a Netanya hotel. Thirty people were murdered and 140 injured, the worst attack of that period.

Some Israelis began to talk about unilateral disengagement from the Palestinians as a way of preventing these horrific killings. I even signed a petition to that effect. Little did I know that it would lead to the building of the separation wall. The ostensible purpose of building the wall was to keep out as many terrorists as possible.

As the wall was being built, the route sometimes involved serious violations of the human rights of Palestinian villagers around Jerusalem. We – left-wing Jews in Jerusalem – were invited by our neighbors in the village of Jabel Mukaber to demonstrate with them. I went there with friends, and one of the residents told us that his mother lives on the other side of the village. Under present circumstances, he can get into his car and within five minutes, show up at her home. If the planned route of the wall is carried out, the village will be split in half and it will take him about three hours to visit his mom. That seemed very unfair.

It in no way at all justifies the use of slogans such "Abu Dis=Warsaw Ghetto" and others that have been painted as graffiti on the wall. In the Warsaw Ghetto, the mother would have been taken away to be gassed. The Occupation is very bad, and must be ended, but it isn't a Holocaust.

I don't know if it reflected our and others' protest, but the Supreme Court in Israel voted to change the route of the wall. During the year of 2004–5, they decided that the route must reflect a balance between the legitimate security needs of Israelis and the human rights of Palestinians. The route indeed was changed, and the folks in Jabel Mukaber invited us back to celebrate. We went another time; this time, there was a lovely concert with children's choirs. A statistic has been quoted that the rate of terror incidents plummeted by over 80% with the building of the wall. The problem with that statistic, encouraging as it is, is that it doesn't take into account other factors that helped, besides the wall, for example the ongoing security coordination and cooperation between Israel and the Palestinian Authority.

Unfortunately, the story doesn't end here. In March of 2008, a Palestinian gunman was driven into the heart of West Jerusalem. He entered the *Merkaz HaRav Yeshiva* at dinner time and killed eight boys, aged 15 to 26, in the dining room, before the security guard finally killed him. Now, I have to explain that with regard to religion, politics, and feminism, I have very little in common with this particular Yeshiva. But just because we are ideologically at odds doesn't mean that I deny their inalienable right to live and practice as they choose.

From what community did this Palestinian gunman come? You guessed it – from Jabel Mukaber . . . I didn't know personally any of the families who lost sons during that awful incident. But if I had, and if I had paid a condolence call, what would I have said to the bereaved parents: "I demonstrated for the right of the people of Jabel Mukaber to freedom of movement?" I'm not in any way suggesting that the village is full of terrorists. But in addition to the gunman there was at least one accomplice, who drove him into town.

And, then, tragically, in November of 2014, two young men from Jabel Mukaber traveled into a West Jerusalem neighborhood, called Har Nof, full of ultra-Orthodox Jews. They entered a synagogue during the morning prayers, brutally murdering four Jewish worshippers and a Druze security man. For some people, this incident was a turning point in their whole relationship with the terrorism perpetrated against us. The blood-stained prayer shawls raised images for them of antisemitic pogroms carried out in Europe. It reminded me of the bombing in the hotel on Seder night.

Some of the residents of Har Nof as quoted in the media expressed surprise that their community would be the locus for such an attack. After all, they explained, many of them are not Zionist and do not serve in the Army. The attackers from Jabel Mukaber were conflating Zionism with Judaism.

I beg to differ with a famous phrase often quoted in French: "tout comprendre c'est tout pardoner" [to understand all is to forgive all].

I certainly am in favor of trying to understand the factors that lead to involvement in terror. Perhaps this reflects my training as a sociologist. But I cannot in any way forgive or justify it.

Still, I think that the most painful feature of my life here has been the rise in racist sentiments among Jews. Back in the 80s, when our anti-racism law was enacted, I thought that was a truly sad day in Israeli history. How, I asked myself, can Jews become racists, having been the number one target of racism ourselves? I didn't realize that things would just get sadder. This particular strand of Jewish racism goes back at least to the late 1960s and the followers of Meir Kahane. They had always been a marginal phenomenon, but now the mainstream seems to be approaching them – or, at least, some of their views – especially within the Orthodox Jewish community.

There is so much delegitimization and even demonization of Israel that I don't want to add to it. I am still a Zionist and I don't believe that Zionism is the root of all evil. I have seen the UN declare that Zionism is racism and then rescind that declaration. I have never supported the settlements, but even the people who do must be enlisted in the struggle against racism. A very good example of this is Israeli president Reuven Rivlin, a right-winger who has taken courageous positions against racism and incitement.

Why do I call myself a "hopeful" pessimist? First, I have lived long enough to know that things change, sometimes unexpectedly, and that situations rarely remain static, for better and for worse. Many people say that the essence of wisdom is the awareness that "this, too, shall pass." If more young people knew that, there might be less teenage suicide.

I have lived to see the Berlin Wall come down and a black man get elected – not once, but twice – to the American Presidency. Perhaps I'll even live to see a woman in that position. I certainly have lived to see major changes in the role of women within Judaism.

Secondly, I quoted earlier Bishop Munib Younan who said, "As long as you believe in a living God, you must have hope." One of the major messages of the Exodus from Egypt is that just because a people have been enslaved for hundreds of years, this doesn't mean they can't be liberated overnight. Rabbi David Hartman called the God of Israel a "God of surprises."

I believe that the pursuit of peace is a religious imperative – not just a Messianic, end-of-days peace when lions and lambs will lie down together, but a pragmatic and sometimes fragmented this-worldly peace. Rabbi Michael Melchior, who served for ten years in the Knesset and was even a Deputy Cabinet Minister, says, what we need is "a piece of peace."

I know that there are many people who used to support the two-state solution but who have lost all hope for its realization. I haven't yet, partly because I don't really see any alternative. I know that in the Middle Ages, one of the most violent parts of the world was Scandinavia; the Swedes, Danes and Norwegians simply couldn't get along. Now they do – they might make jokes about each other, but they're no longer at war. Neither are France, Germany and the UK, who as recently as the 20th century killed millions of each other's military and civilian populations. I hope that someday we'll look back and say "Arabs and Jews? Palestinians and Israelis? They get along just fine."

One more thought: Naomi Shemer was one of the great ladies of Israeli music – a composer *and* lyricist. In 1994, when I received my Ph.D. from the Hebrew University, she was awarded an honorary doctorate. In the 1970s, she wrote a song called "I haven't loved enough yet . . ." (there's a dance to it) which includes a list of all the things she hasn't done. One line says, "I haven't written my memoirs." Well, I guess I have.

Acknowledgements

I WANT TO THANK all of the many people who have helped me
in my life, but more specifically, those who helped me with this
book project: Ruth Berlinger and Professor Celia Deutsch,
NDS, for their encouragement; Dr. Bill Taeusch for his close, care-
ful reading of the first draft and his helpful comments; JoAnne Ad-
lerstein, Rabbi Amy Eilberg, Dr. Seymour ("Epi") Epstein, Linda
Gradstein, Ambassador Tova Herzl, Annette Hochstein, Professor
Michael Krupp and Fern Reiss for their advice; Merav (Cohen) Ci-
dor and Noomi Stahl for reading an early version of the text. Robert
Ellsberg, Blu Greenberg and Dr. Aviva Zornberg gave generously
of their time to read the manuscript and write endorsements.

I wish to express a deep debt of gratitude to my sister, Judy Cohen,
and my brother-in-law, Professor Mayer Gruber, for their generous
support towards the publication of the book.

A heart-felt thank-you also to Tzvi Mauer at Urim Publications, and
his staff: Michal Alatin, Beth Berman, and Sarit Newman.

Throughout the text I have used some people's full names and some
people's first names only. In a few cases, I referred to them as "a friend."
Many people I like or love do not appear. This is only because I didn't
include a specific story about them.

What I have not generally done is to use the traditional phrases, "of
blessed memory" or "peace be upon her" with regard to the deceased.
My decision to write this way reflects an awareness that as time goes
by, more and more of the people in the text will be leaving this world,

but in most cases, the story about them occurred during their lifetimes. I apologize to any who might find this offensive.

The front cover shows me giving a book to Pope Francis in the summer of 2015, at a special audience with about 250 members of the ICCJ. The book is *Building Bridges*, the autobiography of Dr. Victor Goldbloom, a man who preceded me by many years as the president of the organization and was later made a Papal Knight. In February of 2016, Victor died of a heart attack at the age of 92. Having read and enjoyed his memoirs, I thought he might be able to read mine. Unfortunately, that won't happen.

Appendix A

TEN POINTS OF SEELISBERG

1. Remember that One God speaks to us all through the Old and the New Testaments.

2. Remember that Jesus was born of a Jewish mother of the seed of David and the people of Israel, and that His everlasting love and forgiveness embraces His own people and the whole world.

3. Remember that the first disciples, the apostles and the first martyrs were Jews.

4. Remember that the fundamental commandment of Christianity, to love God and one's neighbor, proclaimed already in the Old Testament and confirmed by Jesus, is binding upon both Christians and Jews in all human relationships, without any exception.

5. Avoid distorting or misrepresenting biblical or post biblical Judaism with the object of extolling Christianity.

6. Avoid using the word Jews in the exclusive sense of the enemies of Jesus, and the words 'the enemies of Jesus' to designate the whole Jewish people.

7. Avoid presenting the Passion in such a way as to bring the odium of the killing of Jesus upon all Jews or upon Jews alone. It was only a section of the Jews in Jerusalem who demanded the death of Jesus, and the Christian message has always been that it was the sins of mankind which were exemplified by those Jews and the sins in which all men share that brought Christ to the Cross.

8. Avoid referring to the scriptural curses, or the cry of a raging mob:

"His blood be upon us and our children," without remembering that this cry should not count against the infinitely more weighty words of our Lord: "Father forgive them for they know not what they do."

9. Avoid promoting the superstitious notion that the Jewish people are reprobate, accursed, reserved for a destiny of suffering.
10. Avoid speaking of the Jews as if the first members of the Church had not been Jews.

A Time for Recommitment – The Twelve Points of Berlin:
   A Call to Christian and Jewish Communities Worldwide
We, the International Council of Christians and Jews and our member orga-
nizations, resolve to renew our engagement with the Ten Points of Seelisberg
that inspired our beginnings. Therefore, we issue these calls to Christians,
Jews, and all people of good will:

A Call to Christians and Christian Communities
We commit ourselves to the following goals and invite all Christians and
Christian communities to join us in the continuing effort to remove all vestiges
of contempt towards Jews and enhance bonds with the Jewish communities
worldwide.

1. To combat religious, racial and all other forms of antisemitism
Biblically
a.   By recognizing Jesus' profound identity as a Jew of his day, and interpreting
     his teachings within the contextual framework of first-century Judaism.
b.   By recognizing Paul's profound identity as a Jew of his day, and interpreting
     his writings within the contextual framework of first-century Judaism.
c.   By emphasizing that recent scholarship on both the commonality and
     gradual separation of Christianity and Judaism is critical for our basic
     understanding of the Jewish-Christian relationship.
d.   By presenting the two Testaments in the Christian Bible as complemen-
     tary and mutually affirming rather than antagonistic or inferior/superior.

Denominations that use lectionaries are encouraged to choose and link biblical texts that offer such an affirming theology.

e. By speaking out against Christian misreadings of biblical texts regarding Jews and Judaism that can provoke caricatures or animosity.

Liturgically

a. By highlighting the connection between Jewish and Christian liturgy.

b. By drawing upon the spiritual richness of Jewish interpretations of the scriptures.

c. By cleansing Christian liturgies of anti-Jewish perspectives, particularly in preaching, prayers and hymns.

Catechistically

a. By presenting the Christian-Jewish relationship in positive tones in the education of Christians of all ages, underlining the Jewish foundations of Christian belief and accurately describing the ways Jews themselves understand their own traditions and practices. This includes the curricula of Christian schools, seminaries and adult education programs.

b. By promoting awareness of the long-lived traditions of Christian anti-Judaism and providing models for renewing the unique Jewish-Christian relationship.

c. By underscoring the immense religious wealth found in the Jewish tradition, especially by studying its authoritative texts.

2. To promote inter-religious dialogue with Jews

a. By understanding dialogue as requiring trust and equality among all participants and rejecting any notion of convincing others to accept one's own beliefs.

b. By appreciating that dialogue encourages participants to examine critically their own perceptions of both their own tradition and that of their dialogue partners in the light of a genuine engagement with the other.

3. To develop theological understandings of Judaism that affirm its distinctive integrity

a. By eliminating any teachings that Christians have replaced Jews as a people in covenant with God.

b. By emphasizing the common mission of Jews and Christians in preparing the world for the kingdom of God or the Age to Come.

c. By establishing equal, reciprocal working relationships with Jewish religious and civic organizations.

d. By ensuring that emerging theological movements from Asia, Africa and Latin America, and feminist, liberationist or other approaches integrate an accurate understanding of Judaism and Christian-Jewish relations into their theological formulations.

e. By opposing organized efforts at the conversion of Jews.

4. To pray for the peace of Jerusalem

a. By promoting the belief in an inherent connectedness between Christians and Jews.

b. By understanding more fully Judaism's deep attachment to the Land of Israel as a fundamental religious perspective and many Jewish people's connection with the State of Israel as a matter of physical and cultural survival.

c. By reflecting on ways that the Bible's spiritual understanding of the land can be better incorporated into Christian faith perspectives.

d. By critiquing the policies of Israeli and Palestinian governmental and social institutions when such criticism is morally warranted, at the same time acknowledging both communities' deep attachment to the land.

e. By critiquing attacks on Zionism when they become expressions of antisemitism.

f. By joining with Jewish, Christian and Muslim peace workers, with Israelis and Palestinians, to build trust and peace in a Middle East where all can live secure in independent, viable states rooted in international law and guaranteed human rights.

g. By enhancing the security and prosperity of Christian communities both in Israel and Palestine.

h. By working for improved relations among Jews, Christians and Muslims in the Middle East and the rest of the world.

A Call to Jews and Jewish Communities

We commit ourselves to the following goals and invite all Jews and Jewish communities to join us in the continuing effort to remove all vestiges of animosity and caricature toward Christians and to enhance bonds with Christian churches of the world.

5. **To acknowledge the efforts of many Christian communities in the late 20th century to reform their attitudes toward Jews**

   a. By learning about these reforms through more intensive dialogue with Christians.

   b. By discussing the implications of changes in Christian churches regarding Jews and their understandings of Judaism.

   c. By teaching Jews of all ages about these changes, both in the context of the history of Jewish-Christian relations and according to the appropriate stage of education for each group.

   d. By including basic and accurate background information about Christianity in the curricula of Jewish schools, rabbinic seminaries and adult education programs.

   e. By studying the New Testament both as Christianity's sacred text and as literature written to a large degree by Jews in an historical-cultural context similar to early rabbinic literature, thereby offering insight into the development of Judaism in the early centuries of the Common Era.

6. **To re-examine Jewish texts and liturgy in the light of these Christian reforms**

   a. By grappling with Jewish texts that appear xenophobic or racist, realizing that many religious traditions have uplifting, inspirational texts as well as problematic ones. The emphasis for all religious traditions should be on texts that promote tolerance and openness.

   b. By placing problematic texts within their historical context, in particular writings from the times when Jews were a powerless, persecuted and humiliated minority.

   c. By addressing the possible re-interpretation, change or omission of parts of Jewish liturgy that treat others in problematic ways.

7. **To differentiate between fair-minded criticism of Israel and antisemitism**

   a. By understanding and promoting biblical examples of just criticism as expressions of loyalty and love.

   b. By helping Christians appreciate that communal identity and interconnectedness are intrinsic to Jewish self-understanding, in addition to religious faith and practice, therefore making the commitment to the survival and security of the State of Israel of great importance to most Jews.

8. To offer encouragement to the State of Israel as it works to fulfil the ideals stated in its founding documents, a task Israel shares with many nations of the world

a. By ensuring equal rights for religious and ethnic minorities, including Christians, living within the Jewish state.

b. By achieving a just and peaceful resolution of the Israeli-Palestinian conflict.

A Call to Both Christian and Jewish Communities and Others

We commit ourselves to the following goals and invite Jews, Christians and Muslims, together with all people of faith and goodwill, always to respect the other and to accept each other's differences and dignity.

9. To enhance inter-religious and intercultural education

a. By combating negative images of others, teaching the foundational truth that each human being is created in the image of God.

b. By making the removal of prejudices against the other a high priority in the educational process.

c. By encouraging mutual study of religious texts, so that Jews, Christians, Muslims and members of other religious groups can learn both from and with each other.

d. By supporting common social action in the pursuit of common values.

10. To promote inter-religious friendship and cooperation as well as social justice in the global society

a. By rejoicing in the uniqueness of each person, and promoting everyone's political, economic and social well-being.

b. By recognizing as equal citizens members of faith traditions who have migrated to new homelands where they may have become part of a religious minority.

c. By striving for equal rights for all people, regardless of their religion, gender or sexual orientation.

d. By recognizing and grappling with the fact that feelings of religious superiority – and an accompanying sense that other religions are inferior – are present in each tradition, including one's own.

11. To enhance dialogue with political and economic bodies

a. By collaborating with political and economic bodies whenever possible to promote interreligious understanding.

b. By benefiting from political and economic groups' growing interest in inter-religious relations.

c. By initiating discussion with political and economic bodies around the urgent need for justice in the global community.

12. To network with all those whose work responds to the demands of environmental stewardship

a. By fostering commitment to the belief that every human being is entrusted with the care of the Earth.

b. By recognizing the shared Jewish and Christian biblical duty toward creation, and the responsibility to bring it to bear in public discourse and action.

To all these challenges and responsibilities, we – the International Council of Christians and Jews and its member organizations – commit ourselves.

Berlin, Germany,
July 2009
At the International Conference
and the Annual General Meeting of
the International Council of Christians and Jews

Appendix C

YEDIDYA STATEMENT OF PRINCIPLES

(1) *"In all your ways acknowledge Him . . ."* (Proverbs 3:6)
Kehillat Yedidya supports the concept of full Jewish life according to the *Halacha*. The commandments develop relationships with God, interpersonal relationships, and responsibilities towards the surrounding society.

(2) *"That which is old should be renewed; that which is new should be hallowed."* (Rav Kook)
A life of *Torah* and commandments must never become ossified. We aspire to integrate tradition and changing social reality, within the framework of *Halacha*. The community itself has an important role to play in questions of determining what our customs will be. The life of the community is based on praying together regularly. But the element of *keva*, of fixed prayer, should be infused with *kavana*, intention and meaning. Public prayer should become a spiritual and esthetic experience, with maximum participation. An important component of the services is the *divrei Torah* and *shiurim*, which add an intellectual dimension to the experience.

(3) *"Its ways are ways of pleasantness, and all its paths are peace."* (Proverbs 3:17)
The Torah inculcates within us the pursuit of peace – domestic peace, societal peace, peace among nations. The use of "ways" instead of "way" or "paths" instead of "path" teaches us that within the framework of

Torah, *Halacha* and the community, there may be many different points of view. Even when there is controversy, there should be mutual respect.

(4) "*In the image of God created He him, male and female created He them.*" (Gen. 1:27)
All human beings were created in the image of God and are, therefore, equal. This equality involves men and women, Jews and non-Jews, people with special needs, etc. The synagogue should be open and accessible to all, although equality is not synonymous with sameness. We respect the differences among people and believe that every human being is entitled to the dignity of a creature created in the Divine Image. *Kehillat Yedidya* is recognized as a pioneer in the full involvement of women in community activity.

(5) "*Justice justice shall you pursue . . .*" (Deut. 16:20)
A life of Torah should be based on honesty, moral rectitude and a passion for justice, both on the personal and social levels. We are especially called upon to seek justice for those in our society who are weak and unprotected. As a community, we aspire to express these values in our lives.

(6) "*Do not separate yourself from the community.*" (*Avot* 2:5)
Yedidya is not only a synagogue. It is a true community, in which the members share the happy occasions of all, as well as the problems and pain. Members of *Yedidya* are invested in developing a strong community, characterized by a shared communal culture and mutual aid. Still, we must not forget that we are part of the neighborhood of Bak'a. At the top of our concerns should be the welfare of our neighborhood and our city. We should be involved in the social and cultural life of the neighborhood. In another sense, we are part of the wider religious Zionist community in Israel, Israeli society in general, world Jewry, and the "family" of humankind. Each of these levels brings with it differing degrees of involvement and responsibility.

(7) "*Hospitality is greater than receiving the Divine Presence.*" (*Shabbat* 127a)
We are commanded to offer hospitality to new members of the community, students, new immigrants, and non-Jewish guests, who are interested in experiencing a Shabbat or *Chag* with a Jewish community.

We try to ensure that our guests will feel comfortable at the service and at the Kiddush. Since many of our members are immigrants – new or veteran – the community largely functions for them as a kind of "extended family." This is expressed through an extensive program of social activities, including communal meals on various occasions.

(8) *"Excellent is study of the Torah together with worldliness . . ."(Avot* 2:2)
We strive to emphasize the importance of the sciences and the arts, together with our study of *Torah*. In our *Torah* study, it is not only permitted but encouraged to integrate many and varied sources, comparative insights and commentators of disparate backgrounds. Works of art have a place of honor on the walls of the synagogue.

(9) *"To be a free people in our land . . ."* (HaTikvah)
We see in the State of Israel the expression of Jewish national sovereignty in this world, and celebrate its independence day with honor and festivity. Similarly, we pray for the welfare of the State and of its soldiers. Our lives as citizens of the State obligate us to protect its peace and security through Army or National Service, for both men and women, and to preserve its character as a Jewish and democratic state.

(10) *"You shall teach them diligently unto your children . . .* (Deut. 6:7)
The next generation is the guarantor of continuity. The community is deeply invested in a program of varied age-appropriate activities for the children. We want the children to feel that they are part of the community. The highlight of this activity is the celebration of a *Bar* or Bat Mitzvah, that leads naturally into the junior congregation, and through that, we hope, to becoming an adult member of the community, or, at least, to maintaining a strong, ongoing connection with the community and its values.

Appendix D

In the name of the Faculty and the Board of Governors of the Hebrew Union College-Jewish Institute of Religion, we hereby confer the degree of Doctor of Humane Letters, *honoris causa*, on Dr. Deborah Weissman:

- Innovative educator, sociologist and pioneer of orthodox feminism
- Whose teaching and writing have shed new light and brought new understanding to the social history of Jewish women's education
- Who has taught at and led prestigious institutions impacting Jewish Education in Israel and in the Diaspora
- Whose commitment to dialogue between people of faith has inspired students and colleagues for decades
- And who as the former president of the International Council of Christians and Jews became the first Jewish woman to occupy this important role